PERSONAL WORK

PART I OF

How to Work for Christ

A Compendium of Effective Methods

R. A. TORREY

FLEMING H. REVELL COMPANY

Contents

NOTE

This volume on *Personal Work* is Part I of the author's more comprehensive book entitled *How to Work for Christ*. It is presented in this form for special use as a textbook.

CHAPTER I

THE IMPORTANCE AND ADVANTAGES OF PERSONAL WORK

In our study of the various forms of Christian activity, we begin with "Personal Work," that hand-to-hand dealing with men, women and children. We begin with it because it is the simplest form of Christian work, the kind that every one can do. It is also the most effective method of winning lost souls. The Apostle Peter was brought to Jesus by the hand-to-hand work of his brother Andrew. Andrew first found Christ himself, then he went to Peter quietly and told him of his great find, and thus he led Peter to the Saviour he himself had found. I do not know that Andrew ever preached a sermon; if he did it is not recorded; but he did a great day's work when he led his brother Peter to Jesus. Peter preached a sermon that led to the conversion of 3,000 people, but where would Peter's great sermon have been if Andrew had not first led him to Christ by quiet personal work? Mr. Edward Kimball, a Boston business man, led D. L. Moody, the young Boston shoe clerk, to the Saviour. Where would all Mr. Moody's wonderful work for Christ have been if he himself had not been led to the Saviour by the faithful personal work of his Sunday school teacher? I believe in preaching. It is a great privilege to preach the Gospel, but this world can be reached and evangelized far more quickly and thoroughly by personal work than by public preaching. Indeed, it can be reached and evangelized only by personal work. When the whole church of Jesus Christ shall rouse to its responsibility and privilege in this matter, and every individual Christian become a personal worker, the evangelization of the world will be close at hand. When the membership of any local church shall rouse to its responsibility and privilege in this matter, and each member become a personal worker in the power of the Holy Spirit, a great revival will be close at hand for the community in which that church is located. Personal work is a work that wins but little applause from men, but it accomplishes great things for God.

There are many who think personal work beneath their dignity and their gifts. A blind woman once came to me and said, "Do you think that my blindness will hinder me from working for the Master?" "Not at all; it may be a great help to you, for others seeing your blindness will come and speak to you, and then you will have an opportunity of giving your testimony for Christ, and of leading them to the Saviour." "Oh, that is not what I want," she replied. "It seems to me a waste of time when one might be speaking to five or six hundred at once, just to be speaking to an individual." I answered that our Lord and Saviour Jesus Christ was able to speak to more than five thousand at once, and yet He never thought personal work beneath His dignity or His gifts. Indeed, it was the work the Saviour loved to do. We have more instances of our Saviour's personal work recorded in the Gospels than of His preaching. The one who is above personal work is above his Master.

Its Advantages.

Let us look at the advantages of personal work.

1. *All can do it.* In an average congregation there are not more than four or five who can preach to edification. It would be a great pity, too, should all attempt to become preachers; it would be a great blessing if all would become personal workers. Any child of God can do personal work, and all can learn to do effective personal work. The mother who is confined at home by multiplicity of home duties can still do personal work, first of all with her own children, and then with the servants in the home, with the butcher, the grocer, the tramp who calls at the door, in fact, with everybody who comes within reach. I once knew a mother very gifted in the matter of bringing her own children up in the nurture and admonition of the Lord, who lamented that she could not do some work for Christ. I watched this woman carefully, and found that almost every one who came to the house in any capacity was spoken to about the Saviour, and she was, in point of fact, doing

more for Christ in the way of direct evangelistic work than most pastors.

Even the one shut up at home by sickness can do personal work. As friends come to the sick bed, a word of testimony can be given for Christ, or even an extended conversation can be held. A little girl of twelve, the child of very poor parents, lay dying in the city of Minneapolis. She let her light shine for the Master, and spoke among others to a godless physician, to whom, perhaps, no one else had ever spoken about Christ. A poor girl in New York City, who was rescued from the slums and died a year or two afterwards, was used of God to lead about one hundred men and women to Christ, while lying upon her dying bed.

Even the servant girl can do effective personal work. Lord Shaftesbury, the great English philanthropist, was won to Christ in a godless home by the effective work of a nurse girl.

Traveling men have unusually good opportunities for doing personal work, as they travel on the trains from town to town, as they stop in one hotel after another and go from store to store. A professional nurse once came into my Bible class in Chicago, and at the close of the meeting approached me and said: "I was led to Christ by Mr. —— [a traveling man connected with a large wholesale house]. I was in a hotel parlor, and this gentleman saw me and walked across the parlor and asked me if I was a Christian, and when I told him I was not, he proceeded at once to show me the way of life. I was so startled and impressed to find a traveling man leading others to Christ that I accepted Him as my Saviour then and there. He told me if I ever came to Chicago to come to your Bible class." I have watched this woman for years since, and she herself is a most devoted Christian and effective worker.

How enormous and wonderful and glorious would be the results if all Christians should begin to be active personal workers to the extent of their ability! Nothing else would do so much to promote a revival in any community, and in the land at large. Every pastor should urge this duty upon his people, train them for it, and see that they do it.

2. *It can be done anywhere.* There are but few places where one can preach. There is no place where one cannot do personal

work. How often, as we pass factories, engine houses, lodging houses and other places where crowds are gathered, do we wish that we might get into them and preach the Gospel, but generally this is impossible, but it is altogether possible to go in and do personal work. Furthermore, we can do personal work on the street, whether street meetings are allowed or not. We can do personal work in the homes of the poor and in the homes of the rich, in hospitals, workhouses, jails, station houses, and all sorts of institutions—in a word, everywhere.

3. *It can be done at any time.* The times when we can have preaching services and Sunday schools are quite limited. As a rule, in most communities, we cannot have services more than two or three days in the week, and only three or four hours in the day, but personal work can be done seven days in the week, and any time of day or night. Some of the best personal work done in this country in the last twenty years has been done on the streets at midnight and after midnight. Those who love souls have walked the streets looking for wanderers, and have gone into dens of vice seeking the lost sheep, and hundreds upon hundreds of them have thus been found.

4. *It reaches all classes.* There are large classes of men that no other method will reach. There are the shut-ins who cannot get out to church, the street-car men, the policemen, railroad conductors, sleeping-car men, firemen, the very poor and the very rich. Some cannot and others will not attend church or cottage meeting or mission meeting, but personal work can reach them all.

5. *It hits the mark.* Preaching is necessarily general; personal work is direct and personal. There is no mistaking who is meant, there is no dodging the arrow, there is no possibility of giving what is said away to some one else. Many whom even so expert a Gospel preacher as Mr. Moody has missed have been afterwards reached by personal work.

6. *It meets the definite need, and every need of the person dealt with.* Even when men are aroused and convicted, and perhaps converted, by a sermon, personal work is necessary to bring out into clear light and into a satisfactory experience one whom the sermon has thus aroused, convicted and converted.

7. *It avails where other methods fail.* One of my best workers told me a few weeks ago that she had attended church for years, and had wanted to become a Christian. She had listened to some of the best-known preachers, and still was unsaved, but the very first inquiry meeting she went into she was saved because some one came and dealt with her personally.

8. *It produces very large results.* There is no comparison whatever between what will be effected by good preaching and what will be effected by constant personal work. Take a church of one hundred members; such a church under an excellent pastor would be considered as doing an exceptionally good work if on an average fifty were added annually to this membership. But suppose that that church was trained to do personal work, and that fifty of the one hundred members actually went at it. Certainly one a month won to Christ by each one would not be a large average. That would be six hundred a year instead of the fifty mentioned above. A church of many members, with the most powerful preaching possible, that depends upon the minister alone to win men to Christ by his preaching, would not accomplish anything like what would be accomplished by a church with a comparatively poor preacher, where the membership generally were personal workers.

CHAPTER II

THE CONDITIONS OF SUCCESS

I. Personal experimental knowledge of Jesus Christ as Saviour.

The first condition of success in personal work, and in all soul-saving work, is a personal experimental knowledge of Jesus Christ as Saviour. It was because the Apostle Paul could say:

> "This is a faithful saying, and worthy of all acceptation, that Christ Jesus came into the world to save sinners; *of whom I am chief.*" I Tim. 1:15

that he had power in bringing other men to that Saviour. It is the man who knows Jesus as his own Saviour, who will have a longing to bring others to this wonderful Saviour whom he has himself found; and it is the man who knows Jesus as his Saviour who will understand how to bring others to the Saviour whom he has found. There are many to-day who are trying to save others, who are not saved themselves. There are others, who, while they are probably saved men, have such a vague knowledge of Christ as their own Saviour, that they cannot hope to make the way of salvation clear to others.

A personal, experimental knowledge of Jesus Christ as a Saviour includes three things:

1. A knowledge that our own sins have been forgiven because Jesus bore them in His own body on the Cross;

2. A knowledge that the risen Christ is delivering us daily from the power of sin;

3. An absolute surrender of our wills to Jesus Christ as our Lord and Master.

II. Life is clean within and without.

The second condition of success in personal work is really involved in the first, and is a life clean within and without.

14

In II Tim. 2:21 we read,

"If a man therefore purge himself from these, he shall be a vessel unto honour, sanctified, and meet for the master's use, and prepared unto every good work."

If a man is to be used of God, his life must be clean—not only his outward life as the world sees it, but his inward secret life as it is known only to God and to himself. One who holds on to any sin of act or thought or affection cannot expect to have power with a holy God, and consequently cannot expect to have power for God. Many a man and woman of great natural gifts, and unusual knowledge of the Bible, are trying to do work for God and meet with little or no success. People wonder why it is that their work is so devoid of results, but if we knew their secret life as God knows it, we would understand their failure; there is sin before God. It has often been said, and well said, that "God does not demand a beautiful vessel for His work, but He does demand a clean one." Many are working on in disappointment and failure, working hard but accomplishing nothing, because God sees sin in their inner life which they will not give up.

III. Personal work is a surrendered life, a life wholly given up to God.

The third condition of success in personal work is a surrendered life, a life wholly given up to God. Paul was mighty as a worker for Christ because he could say,

"For to me to live is Christ."

The miracle of the five loaves and two fishes (Matt. 14:17–20), is deeply significant. The disciples said unto Jesus, "We have here but five loaves, and two fishes. He said, Bring them hither to me." We are told with a good deal of emphasis upon the definite article, He "took *the* five loaves and *the* two fishes," that is, He took all that they had. It was not much, but they brought it all. Then He blessed it and broke it and there was an abundance for all. But if one of these insignificant barley loaves had been kept back, or one of these little fishes, there would not have been enough to go around. We, too, may not have much, it may be only five barley crackers and two little fishes, but if we will bring them all, absolutely all, to Christ, He will take them, bless them and multiply them; but if we hold back one cracker or one fish, He will not bless and multiply. Here lies the secret of failure in many a one who would work for Christ; there is one cracker kept back, or one little fish. We talk very lightly of absolute surrender to God, but it means more than most people who profess it seem to realize. I would ask each reader of these pages, have you brought all to Christ—absolutely all—absolutely ALL?

IV. Men out of Christ are lost.

The one who would have success in personal work must have a deep realization that men out of Christ are lost. Jesus had this. He said,

> "For the Son of man is come to seek and to save that which was LOST." Luke 19:10.

When He looked upon men living in sin, He knew and realized the utter ruin of their condition. The same thing was true of Paul. We read in Acts 20:31 that he "ceased not to warn every one night and day *with tears.*" He knew that if one had not a saving knowledge of Jesus Christ he was eternally lost. This overwhelming conviction that men and women out of Christ are eternally lost, seems to be very rare in our day, and this is one great reason why so few have real power in soul-winning. How can we get this realization?

1. First of all, by studying what the Bible has to say about the present standing and condition and future destiny of those who are out of Christ.

2. By believing what the Bible says upon these points without trying to tone it down, and make it fit in with the popular notions of the day.

3. By dwelling upon these truths about the lost condition of men out of Christ until they take hold upon our hearts and we realize their meaning. These things are not pleasant to think about, but they are true, and we ought to think about them until our souls are on fire to save men from the awful condition of utter ruin in which they now are, and from the destiny of eternal shame and despair to which they are hurrying.

V. Love.

The fifth condition of success in personal work is love. Nothing wins like love. In the first place it leads to untiring effort for the salvation of others. If I really love men, I cannot bear the thought that they should be lost forever, and I will be willing to work day and night to save them from such an awful destiny. In the second place, love attracts others to us. There is nothing so irresistible as love. It is Jesus Christ lifted up on the Cross, a revelation of God's love and of His own love to man, that draws all men unto Him (Jno. 12:32). Men will not put you off if they really believe that you love them, but they will never believe that you love them unless you really do. We need not only love to men, but love to Christ. It was the love of Christ that constrained Paul to his untiring efforts to bring men to a knowledge of Christ. The great men and women of Christian history have been the men and women who have had a great love to Christ, men and women whose hearts were all aglow with love to the glorious Son of God.

But how can we get love? First of all, by dwelling upon Christ's love to us.

"We love him, because he first loved us." I Jno. 4:19.

We shall never appreciate Christ's love to us until we see it against the black background of our own sin. It is the one who is forgiven much who loves much (Luke 7:47). The one who has never been brought to a deep realization of his own sinfulness before God will have no warmth of love to that Saviour who, by His own atoning death on the Cross, redeemed him from the awful depth to which he had sunk. The Apostle Paul realized that he was the chief of sinners, and that Jesus loved him and gave Himself for him, so he was full of love to Jesus Christ.

"This is a faithful saying, and worthy of all acceptation, that Christ Jesus came into the world to save sinners *of whom I am chief.*" III Tim. 1:15.
"I am crucified with Christ; nonetheless I live; yet not I, but Christ liveth in me; and the life which I now live in the flesh I live by the faith of the Son of God, who *loved me, and gave himself for me.*" Gal. 2:20.

If we are to have love to Christ and love to men, the Holy Ghost must impart it. The first fruit of the Spirit is love:

"But the fruit of the Spirit is *love,* joy, peace, longsuffering, gentleness, goodness, faith." Gal. 5:22.

If we will look to the Holy Spirit to do His whole work in our hearts, He will soon fill them with love to Christ and love to our fellow men.

VI. Perseverance.

The sixth condition of success in personal work is perseverance. No work requires so much patience and perseverance as soul-winning. Men are not usually won to Christ in a day. You must hold on to men day after day, week after week, month after month, and if need be, year after year. You must not give them up even though you seem to make absolutely no headway at first, and even though you seem to do more harm than good. When you start out to lead a man to Christ, keep after that man until he is saved, no matter how long it takes. Study how to get at men who are unreachable. Men who cannot be reached in one way can in another. There are very few men in the world to whose hearts there is not an open door somewhere, if only we will search diligently until we find it. If we cannot get in at the door, perhaps we can break up the roof and get in that way. Any one who wishes to win souls at the rate of one every fifteen minutes had better go into some other business. Take time; never give up; and do thorough work. I waited and watched fifteen long years to get my chance with one man. Never a day passed for all those fifteen years that I did not speak to God about that man. At last my chance came, and it was my privilege to lead him to Christ. He afterwards became a preacher of the Gospel, and is now in heaven. I was with him the day before he died, and shall never forget that day as long as I live. When you undertake to bring a man to Christ, never give up.

VII. Practical knowledge of the Bible.

The seventh condition of success in personal work is a practical knowledge of the Bible.

> "Every Scripture inspired of God is also profitable for teaching, for reproof, for correction, for instruction which is in righteousness: that the man of God may be complete, *furnished completely unto every good work.*" II Tim. 3:16, 17, R.V.

In the Bible is all the truth we need in dealing with men. The Word of God is the only instrument that God has appointed for the salvation of men, and the only instrument He honors is the Word. It is the Word that produces conviction of sin. It is the Word that regenerates. It is the Word that produces faith:

"Now when they heard this, they were *pricked in their heart,* and said unto Peter and to the rest of the apostles, Men and brethren, what shall we do?" Acts 2:37.

"Being *born again,* not of corruptible seed but of incorruptible, by *the Word of God,* which liveth and abideth for ever." I Pet. 1:23.

"So then faith cometh by hearing, and hearing by *the Word of God.*" Rom. 10:17.

If then we are to be used in soul-winning, we must know the Bible. There are five texts that ought to sink deep into the heart of every personal worker. They are:

1. "So then faith cometh by hearing, and hearing by *the Word of God.*" Rom. 10:17.

2. "The seed is *the Word of God.*" Luke 8:11.

3. "Being born again, not of corruptible seed, but of incorruptible, by *the Word of God,* which liveth and abideth for ever." I Pet. 1:23.

4. "And take the helmet of salvation, and the sword of the Spirit, *which is the Word of God.*" Eph. 6:17.

5. "Is not *my Word like as a fire?* said the Lord; and *like a hammer* that breaketh the rock in pieces?" Jer. 23:29.

The personal worker who depends upon any instrument other than the Word of God is doomed to failure. But we must have a practical knowledge of the Bible, that is we must know how to use it for definite results. A great many men have a large theoretical knowledge of the Bible, but no practical knowledge. They do not know how to use the Bible so as to accomplish anything definite by its use. In an inquiry meeting one evening, I asked one of the best Bible scholars in America to speak to an inquirer and show her the way of life, and he whispered in my ear, "I don't know how to do that." A small practical knowledge of the Bible is better in personal work than a large theoretical knowledge. A practical knowledge of the Bible involves four things:

1. A knowledge how to so use the Bible as to show men, and make men realize, their need of a Saviour.

2. A knowledge of how to use the Bible so as to show men Jesus as just the Saviour who meets their need.

3. A knowledge of how to use the Bible so as to show men how to make Jesus their own Saviour.

4. A knowledge of how to use the Bible so as to meet the difficulties that stand in the way of their accepting Christ.

A large part of the following pages will be devoted to imparting this particular kind of Bible knowledge.

VIII. Prayer.

The eighth condition of success in personal work is prayer. God honors prayer. In nothing does He honor it more than in the matter of soul-winning. The one who is to be much used of God in soul-winning, must spend much time in prayer. There are four things for which we must especially pray:

1. We must ask God to bring to us, or us to, the right persons. We cannot speak with every one. If we attempt it, we will spend much time in speaking where we can do no good, that we might have used in speaking where we could have accomplished something for Christ. God alone knows the one to whom He intends us to speak, and we must ask Him to point him out to us, and expect Him to do it.

"Then *the Spirit said unto Philip,* Go near, and join thyself to *this* chariot." Acts 8:29.

2. We should ask God to give us the right message in each case where we do speak with any one. We can learn much by studying what is the right message for any given class of men, but after all our study, we must look directly to God for the right message in each individual case. Many cases will baffle us, but no case will baffle God. We need and must have the direct guidance of the Holy Spirit in each individual case. Every experienced worker could testify to many instances in which God has led him to use some text of Scripture that he would not otherwise have used, but which proved to be just the one needed.

3. We must pray God to give power to that which He has given us to say. We need not only a message from God, but power from God to send the message home. Most workers have to learn this lesson by humiliating experiences. They sit down beside an unsaved person and reason, and plead, and bring forth texts from the Word of God, but the man does not accept Christ. At last it dawns upon them that they are trying to convert the man in their own strength, and they lift a short but humble prayer to God for His strength, and in a very little while this "very difficult case" has settled the matter and is rejoicing in Christ.

4. We must pray to God to carry on the work after we have done everything in our power, and our work has come to an end.

After having done that which seems to have been our whole duty in any given instance, whatever may have been the apparent result of our work, whether successful or unsuccessful, we should definitely commit the case to God in prayer. If there is anything the average worker in this hurrying age needs to have impressed upon him, it is the necessity of much prayer. By praying more, we will not work any less, and we will accomplish vastly more.

IX. Baptism with the Holy Ghost.

The ninth condition of success in personal work is the baptism with the Holy Ghost. In Acts 1:8 we read,

> "But ye *shall receive power*, after that the Holy Ghost is come upon you."

The supreme condition of power in the apostolic church was the definite baptism with the Holy Ghost. The supreme condition of success in soul-winning is the same to-day. Many in these days are trying to prove that there is no such thing as a special baptism with the Holy Spirit, but a candid and careful study of the Acts of the Apostles will show that there is. Very many in our day also know by blessed experience that the baptism with the Holy Spirit is a present day reality. One ounce of believing experience along this line is worth whole tons of unbelieving exegesis, no matter how subtle and learned it may be. There are thousands of men and women in this and other lands who have been brought out of a place of powerlessness into a place of power in the Lord's service, through meeting the conditions plainly laid down in the Bible for receiving the Holy Ghost. This baptism with the Holy Spirit is for every child of God, and the one who would be largely used of God in personal work must get it at any cost.

CHAPTER III

WHERE TO DO PERSONAL WORK

I. Personal work after a Gospel Meeting.

Perhaps the easiest and most natural place to do personal work is after a Gospel meeting. Whenever you attend a meeting, watch for some one to deal with after the meeting is over. Do not trust to chance in the matter, but as the minister preaches the sermon keep your eyes on the audience and watch who it is that is hit and what hits them, then you can follow up the work that the minister has already done by his sermon. You will soon acquire good judgment in deciding with whom it is wisest to speak. Of course one must be on his guard against being obtrusive in watching others. Before you go to the meeting pray definitely to God to give you some one at the meeting, and then watch for an answer to your prayer. When you have found your man, go for him, and do not let him slip away under any consideration. It is often well to go as quickly as possible to one of the doors of the meeting-house, and without making oneself too prominent, watch people as they come out, and then gently and courteously approach some one, and deal with him about his soul.

There is a great difference in Christian workers. Some seem never to get any one at the close of a meeting unless some one else takes them to them. They wait around with their Bible under their arm for some one to come to them and take them to an inquirer; others keep their eyes open for themselves, and almost always manage to get hold of some one.

In many of the more active churches, the church is divided into sections with an overseer over each division of the church, and individual workers under the overseer. This is an excellent plan. When it is well carried out it prevents any hopeful cases from getting out without being dealt with personally.

II. In homes.

The Apostle Paul tells us that he preached the Gospel not only publicly, but "from house to house" (Acts 20:20). There is far too little Christian work done in the home. The best home to begin with is your own. Jesus bade the demoniac of Gadara when he was healed to return to his own house and show how great things God had done unto him (Luke 8:39). Every man who is converted should begin to tell the saving power of Christ first in his own home, to his own relatives and friends. Many a mother with her family of children regrets that she has not a wider field of labor for Christ, but she will find one of the grandest of all fields in her own home.

But we should not limit our personal work to our own homes; we should do it in the homes where we visit. In this way those who make us partakers of their hospitality will entertain angels unawares (Heb. 13:2). A godly man who once visited in the home of Spurgeon's parents, by a few words to the little boy, made an impression upon that boy that went far toward making him the mighty minister of the Gospel that he became in after years.

Then we should do personal work in the houses that we enter in our house-to-house visitation. That man or woman is a poor church visitor who simply makes a pleasant call or talks upon religious generalities. The true visitor will find frequent opportunities for doing effective personal work with some of the inhabitants of the home, or with strangers they may find calling upon them.

III. On the streets.

Here again we have the Apostle Paul for an example. Not only did he reason "in the synagogue with the Jews and the devout persons," but also "in the market place every day with them that met with him." (Acts 17:17, R.V.) As you walk the streets, be listening for the voice of God to say "Go and speak to that man." Very often as one walks the street of a crowded city or the lonely roads of the country, if he is walking with God, the leading will come to speak to some one that he meets by the way, and countless are the souls that have been led out of darkness into light in this way. As you look upon the surging crowd, ask God if there is some one in this crowd with whom He desires you to speak. Sometimes it is well to stand to one side and watch the people as they pass. Soon there will come a face that interests you, a face it may be that tells a story of sin, or sorrow and need. You can quietly follow this person and watch for an opportunity to engage him in conversation, and then point him to the one who says, "Come unto me, all ye that labor and are heavy laden, and I will give you rest."

IV. In the parks and other resorts.

The parks are often full of people who have plenty of leisure and are willing to talk upon almost any subject. Go through the park and find your man, engage him in a conversation, and as quickly as you can, lead him up to the great subject that is burning in your own heart. Oftentimes it is well to begin to talk about matters of passing interest, the burning questions of the day, then lead by the shortest possible route to the great question. Sometimes show the one with whom you are talking a tract, and ask his opinion of it, and this will lead easily to the matter uppermost in your mind. Not infrequently if you sit down in a park some one will come and sit down beside you and begin to talk to you, then of course it is very easy to lead him into a conversation about his own soul's need.

V. On a walk or ride.

In this we have our Saviour's own example. He made the hearts of the two disciples burn within them while He spoke to them in the way, and opened to them the Scriptures (Luke 24: 32). We also have the example of Philip the evangelist. The Spirit bade him go and join himself to the chariot of Queen Candace's treasurer. The treasurer invited him up into the chariot to ride with him, and the memorable conversation and personal dealing that followed led to the conversion and baptism of the treasurer, and the carrying of the Gospel into Ethiopia (Acts 8:29–38). There are few more favorable places to do personal work than on a walk or ride with a friend or even with a stranger.

VI. At the place of business.

Here again we have the Saviour's example. "As he passed by, he saw Levi the son of Alphaeus sitting at the receipt of custom, and said unto him, Follow me. And he arose and followed him." (Mark 2:14) Of course we ought not to interrupt men and hinder their proper performance of their business duties. Many a workman has rare opportunities to speak with his fellow workmen, sometimes during work hours, sometimes during the noon rest. One of the most earnest Christian ministers I ever knew had been a godless employe in a factory, but the man who worked next to him was a Christian, took an interest in his fellow employe's soul, and was instrumental under God in leading him to Christ. I have met a good many from one of the largest business institutions in our city who have been led to Christ by one consecrated young man in the establishment. This young man has since gone as a foreign missionary, but he was used of God to lead many of his fellow employes to Christ before he went. It is well, wherever possible, to go into stores and factories and other places of business for the deliberate purpose of leading those who work there to Christ. Of course, as already said, it will not do to interrupt a man at his business, neither will it do generally to deal with him when others are around and listening, nor should he be taken at an hour when he is in a bad temper; but one who has that discretion that God is so ready to give (James 1:5) will find many opportunities for doing the Master's work. It is quite possible oftentimes to drop a word, or even to have a little talk, when there is not a great pressure of business, with the clerk who sells us goods, or with the barber who shaves us, or with the boy who blacks our shoes. There are five marks of a good opportunity; when one is alone, unoccupied, in good humor, communicative and in a serious mood.

VII. On cars and boats.

Traveling on a train affords a very rare opportunity for personal work. Travelers usually have much time that hangs heavily upon their hands, and are glad to get into conversation with any one, but if one is a real Christian, there is one subject always uppermost in his mind, one subject that he would rather talk about than any other, and that is Jesus Christ. When you get into a train, get as good a seat for yourself as you can, put your coat and grip out of the way, move away over to the farther side of the seat, and make the vacant space beside you look as inviting as possible. If the car is at all crowded, you will soon have a fellow passenger, and the desired opportunity for personal work. Sometimes it is well to keep your coat and grip in the seat beside you until you see the man or woman that you want coming, and then remove them and move along in a way of silent invitation.

It is well to talk with the trainmen and porters. They are usually willing to talk, and many of them have been led to Christ by Spirit-filled workers who were traveling with them.

Many Christian workers go through trains and give tracts to every one on the train. I am not sure that this is the wisest thing to do, but I know that great blessing has come from it in many cases. Certainly it is well to carry a good supply of religious literature with you when you travel. Some of the books of the Bible Institute Colportage Association are excellent for this purpose, such, e.g., as "Probable Sons." People are willing to read almost anything on a train, and these books without any comment oftentimes will lead the reader to Christ, and when they do not do this, they pave the way for a conversation.

Street cars are not as favorable a place for personal work as trains. One does not have the time or opportunity that he has on a train, and yet good work can be done on a street car, both with the passengers and with the motorman and conductor. A minister once said to me, "I was greatly ashamed last night going down on the street car. I was sitting inside the car talking on unimportant matters with friends, and as I looked to the front end of the car, I saw one member of my church talking with the driver about his soul, and when I looked to the other end of the car I saw another member of my church talking to the conductor, and there I, the pastor of the church, was doing nothing but wasting my time."

VIII. Prisons, hospitals, and other public institutions.

A fine place to do personal work is in public institutions, such as prisons and hospitals, where many people are gathered together and are at leisure from morning till night. Every Sunday, all over this land, devoted men and women are going into prisons, jails and hospitals, carrying the glad tidings of salvation, and thousands are being converted to God through their faithful personal work. Many of the best Christians that I know to-day were brought to Christ in prison, not so much through the public preaching, as through the personal work of some devoted child of God who went from cell to cell and talked to the men about Christ. But while so much is being done already in this direction, there are many prisons and jails and hospitals where little or nothing is done.

Nurses in hospitals have a rare opportunity of doing personal work in the institutions where they are employed. Fortunately a very large proportion of trained nurses are devoted Christian women, and yet many of them do not realize the opportunities that God has put within their reach. A very unusual opportunity is also open to the Christian physician. Indeed a true Christian physician will oftentimes find opportunities for doing personal work that even the minister of the Gospel cannot find. Sometimes it will be with the patient whom he is treating, sometimes with the relatives and friends of the patient who are in deep anxiety as to the outcome of the sickness.

What has been said does not of course cover all the places where personal work can be done, but it will suggest rich fields of opportunity. To put it in a word, personal work should be done everywhere. We read of the early disciples that "they that were scattered abroad went *everywhere* preaching the Word" (Acts 8: 4), that is talking to individuals about Jesus, showing them the word of truth as it is found in the Bible, and leading them to accept it. Every child of God should be at all times on the lookout for opportunities to speak personally to some man or woman about Christ.

CHAPTER IV

HOW TO BEGIN

One of the most difficult points in personal work is beginning. It is comparatively easy to go on after one has got an opening.

I. Find the one to deal with.

The first thing is to find the one to deal with. As has already been said, we should pray God to lead us to some one, or some one to us. When we go to church, or when we walk the street, when we are in the park, or on the train, or calling; in a word, whenever we have time that is not demanded by other duties we should look up to God and definitely ask Him to lead us to the one with whom we are to speak, if it is His will that we employ that time in work for Him. Further than this, we should be on the lookout for opportunities. A fisherman cultivates a keen eye for opportunities to catch fish; and a soul-winner should cultivate a keen eye for opportunities for soul-winning. Whenever we are thrown into the company of a man or woman, the great probability is that it is a providential opening, and we should be ready to meet it as such. It is said of one of the most distinguished Sunday school workers in this country that he makes it a point whenever he is alone with any individual to speak to him about his soul. The story is told of Uncle John Vassar, that being left alone in a hotel parlor with a strange lady, he at once approached her and began to speak to her about her soul. After he had gone, the woman's husband returned, and she told him what had happened. The husband was in a great rage, and said, "If I had been here, I would have sent him about his business." His wife replied, "If you had been here, you would have thought he was about his business." We ought to make soul-winning our business, and improve every possible opportunity.

II. Conversation.

Having found your man, begin a conversation. How shall that be done? In the inquiry room, by asking at once a few leading questions to find out just where the man stands, for example: "Are you a Christian?" "Are you saved?" "Have you been born again?" "Upon what do you base your hope of eternal life?" "Are you confessing Christ openly before the world?" "Have you surrendered all you have and are to Christ?" Sometimes it is well to begin in this direct way even when you meet some one casually. The question "Are you saved?" is as a general rule a better one to ask than "Are you a Christian?" It is more likely to set one to thinking. It is more definite and pointed. Many will take the asking of such a question as an impertinence, but that will not prove that the question has not done good. Not a few people who have become angry at a stranger putting a question like this to them have afterward been converted in consequence of it. There are many other questions that one may ask that will set men to thinking and open the way for further conversation. For example, you can ask a man, "Do you think that life is worth living?" and after you have engaged him in conversation on this point you can lead him on and tell of the life that really is worth living. Or you can ask an utter stranger, "How do you think a man can get the most real satisfaction out of life, that is, of course, by accepting Jesus Christ as a Saviour." Or you can say to a man, "I have learned the great secret of happiness," and when he asks you what it is, you can tell him. Of course these are offered only as suggestions of ways in which to begin a conversation.

A good way to begin is by handing the person with whom you wish to deal, a well-chosen tract to read. When he has finished the tract, you can ask him what he thinks about it, and thus the way is opened to a conversation on the great subject. It is often well to begin by engaging the person in a general conversation, perhaps on subjects quite remote from religion, and gradually working around to the point. It was thus that Christ engaged the woman of Samaria, making a very simple request of her, that she would give Him a drink (Jno. 4:7), but before long, He was telling her of the living water. If the person with whom you wish to deal is older than yourself, you might begin by saying, "There is a subject in which I am deeply interested, and I am trying to get all the light upon it that I can; you are much older than I, and perhaps you can help me; the subject is 'How to Be Saved.'"

Showing people little kindnesses very often opens the way for a conversation on the great subject. For example, in a crowded car one can move along and invite some one who is standing to a seat by his side. It is the most natural thing in the world then to get into conversation, and the favor of the person who has been standing is gained, and it will be very easy to lead on to the great subject. When one is riding, and sees some one else walking, an invitation to the walker to ride will afford a splendid opportunity for approaching him on the subject of his soul's salvation. Mr. Moody made a constant practice of inviting those with whom he wished to deal to go riding with him. As he drew near to some quiet spot, he would speak to them of what was upon his heart, and then stop the horse and have a season of prayer. No one can tell how many were thus led to Christ. Sometimes it is well to show the people that you would lead to Christ kindness for days and weeks, and even years, waiting for your opportunity to say a word. A devoted missionary to China who had made great sacrifices to go to that land was received by the people with bitterest hatred, but he simply gave himself up to live among them and live for them. One by one opportunities came of showing them kindnesses, and after years of self-sacrificing living, he had so won their confidence that it was an easy matter for him to lead them to Christ. But he had to begin by showing them the most ordinary, everyday kindnesses, far away, apparently, from the subject that was closest to his heart.

Sometimes a person's face will tell the story of discontent, unhappiness or unrest. In such a case it is easy to ask the person if he is happy, and when he says no, tell him you can tell him of One who can make him happy if only he will take Him.

Tact in beginning will come with experience, but it is better to begin awkwardly than not to begin at all. I do not think that any one could begin more awkwardly in this work than I did with the first person whom I led to Christ. I felt that God wanted me to speak to this young man, and I called on him for that purpose, but when I met him I had not the slightest idea what to say. I talked on and on waiting for an opportunity, and at last blundered out awkwardly what I had come for. God blessed the awkward but honest effort, and the young man was saved, and has become a very active and efficient worker for Christ.

The best way to learn how to do personal work is by doing it. gaining wisdom from your mistakes.

III. Find out as soon as possible where the person with whom you are dealing stands.

Having begun the conversation, find out as soon as possible where the person with whom you are dealing stands. In order to treat a case intelligently, you need just as much as a physician to know just where the man is at present. But how can we find out to what class any person belongs?

1. First of all, *by asking him questions,* such questions as "Are you saved?" "Have you eternal life?" "Have you been born again?" "Do you know that you are a great sinner before God?" "Do you know that your sins are forgiven?" Or you can ask a person directly, "Where do you stand, what do you believe?" He may answer these questions untruthfully, either from ignorance or a desire to mislead you; nevertheless the answers and his manner of giving them will show you a great deal about his real state.

2. *By watching the inquirer's face.* A man's face will often reveal that which his words try to conceal. Any one who cultivates a study of the faces of those with whom he deals, will soon be able to tell in many instances their exact state irrespective of anything they may say.

3. *By observing his tone and manner.* A man's tone or his manner often tells more than his words. A man who is not saved will very likely tell you that he is, but his tone and manner will reveal plainly that he is not. If one gets angry at you for asking these questions, that of itself reveals an uneasy conscience.

4. *By the Holy Spirit.* The Holy Spirit, if we look to Him to do it, will often flash into our minds a view of the man's position, and just the Scripture that he needs.

IV. Lead him as directly as you can to accept Jesus Christ as a personal Saviour, and to surrender to Him as his Lord and Master.

When we have learned where the person with whom we are dealing stands, the next thing to do is to lead him as directly as we can to accept Jesus Christ as a personal Saviour, and to surrender to Him as his Lord and Master. We must always bear in mind that the primary purpose of our work is not to get people to join the church, or to give up their bad habits, or to do anything else than this, to accept Jesus Christ as their Saviour, the one who bore their sins in His own body on the tree, and the one through whom they can have immediate and entire forgiveness, and as their Master to whom they surrender absolutely the guidance of their thoughts, purposes, feelings and actions.

V. Show him from God's Word that he has forgiveness of sins and eternal life.

Having led any one to thus accept Christ, the next step will be to show him from God's Word that he has forgiveness of sins and eternal life. Acts 10:43; 13:39; John 3:36; 5:24 will answer for this purpose.

VI. Show him how to make a success of the Christian life upon which he has entered.

The next step will be to show him how to make a success of the Christian life upon which he has entered.

CHAPTER V

HOW TO DEAL WITH THOSE WHO REALIZE THEIR NEED OF A SAVIOUR AND REALLY DESIRE TO BE SAVED

We come now to the question of how to deal with individual cases. We begin with those who realize their need of a Saviour, and really desire to be saved. We begin with these because they are the easiest class to deal with.

I. Show them Jesus as a sin-bearer.

The first thing to show one who realizes his need of a Saviour is that Jesus has borne his sins in His own body on the cross. A good verse for this purpose is Is. 53:6:

> "All we like sheep have gone astray; we have turned every one to his own way; and the Lord hath laid on him the iniquity of us all."

Get the inquirer to read the verse himself, then say to him, "The first half of this verse shows you your need of salvation, the second half shows you the provision that God has made for your salvation. Read again the first half of the verse. Is this true of you? Have you gone astray like a sheep? Have you turned to your own way?" "Yes." "Then what are you?" Get the inquirer to say, "I am lost." "We will now look at the provision God has made for your salvation; read the last half of the verse. Who is the one in this verse upon whom our iniquity has been laid?" "Christ." "What then has God done with your sin?" "Laid it on Christ." "Is it then on you any longer?" Go over it again and again until he sees that his sin is not on him, but that it is on Christ, and has been settled forever. I often use a simple illustration in making the meaning of the verse plain. I let my right hand represent the inquirer, my left hand represent Christ, and my Bible represent the inquirer's sin. I first lay the Bible on my right hand and say, "Now where is your sin?" The inquirer replies of course, "On me." I then repeat the last half of the verse, "the Lord hath *laid on him* the iniquity of us all," and transfer the Bible from my right hand to my left, and ask, "Where is your sin now?" The inquirer replies, "On Him, of course." I then ask, "Is it on you any longer?" and he says, "No, on Christ." Very many people have been led out into light and joy by this simple illustration.

I sometimes put it in this way, in using this verse, "There are two things which a man needs to know, and one thing he needs to do in order to be saved. What he needs to know is, first, that he is a lost sinner, and this verse tells him that, and second, that Christ is an all-sufficient Saviour, and this verse tells him that. What he needs to do is to accept this all-sufficient Saviour whom God has provided. Now will you accept Him right here and now?"

Another excellent verse to show Jesus as a sin-bearer, is Gal. 3:13:

"Christ hath redeemed us from the curse of the law, *being made a curse for us:* for it is written, Cursed is every one that hangeth on a tree."

The inquirer should be given the verse to read for himself. When he has read it, you may question him something like this: "What does this verse tell us that Christ has redeemed us from?" "Whom has He redeemed?" "How has He redeemed us from the curse of the law?" "Do you believe that Christ has redeemed you from the curse of the law by being made a curse in your place?" "Will you read it then in the singular instead of in the plural?" Make it clear what you mean, until the inquirer reads the verse in this way: "Christ has redeemed me from the curse of the law, being made a curse for me; for it is written, cursed is every one that hangeth on a tree."

Another good verse for this purpose is II Cor. 5:21:

"For he hath made him to be sin for us, who knew no sin, that we might be made the righteousness of God in him."

Have him read the verse, and then ask questions somewhat as follows: "Who is it that hath been made sin for us?" "For whom has Christ been made sin?" "For what purpose is it that Christ has been made sin for us?" "Can you put this verse in the singular and read it this way: 'For he hath made him to be sin for me, who knew no sin; that I might be made the righteousness of God in him'?"

Sometimes it will be well to use all three of these passages, but as a rule the first is sufficient; so far as my own experience goes, it is more effective than either of the other passages—in fact, I deal with very few men with whom I do not use Is. 53:6 sooner or later.

II. Show them Jesus as a risen Saviour, able to save to the uttermost.

It is not enough to show them Jesus as a sin-bearer, for through believing in Jesus as a sin-bearer one merely gets pardon from sin, but there is something else that the sinner needs, that is deliverance from sin's power. In order to get this, they need to see Jesus as a risen Saviour, able to save to the uttermost. By believing in Christ crucified, we get pardon, but by believing in Christ risen, we get deliverance from sin's power. One of the best verses to use for this purpose is Heb. 7:25:

"Wherefore he is able also to save them to the uttermost that come unto God by him, seeing he ever liveth to make intercession for them."

When the inquirer has read the passage, ask him who it is that is able to save, and to what extent He is able to save. Explain to the inquirer what "to the uttermost" means. Many read this passage as though it taught that Jesus was able to save from the uttermost. This is true, but it is not the truth of this text, it is save *to* the uttermost. Then ask the inquirer why it is that Jesus is able to save to the uttermost. Dwell upon this thought, that *Jesus ever liveth,* that He is not only a Saviour who once died and made atonement for sin, but that He is a Saviour who lives to-day, and is able to keep from sin's power. Then ask the inquirer if he is willing to trust Jesus as a living Saviour, one to whom he can look day by day for victory over sin.

Another good verse to use for this purpose is Jude 24:

"Now unto him that is *able to keep you from falling,* and to present you faultless before the presence of his glory with exceeding joy."

When the inquirer has read the verse, ask him what this verse says Jesus is able to do, emphasize "to keep you from falling." Explain why it is that Jesus is able to keep from falling; because He is a risen, living Saviour to-day, and get the inquirer to see plainly that he is to look to the risen Christ to keep him from falling.

Matt. 28:18 is a good verse to use to bring out the extent of Christ's power:

> "And Jesus came and spake unto them, saying, All power is given unto me in heaven and in earth."

A young convert needs to realize that he is to stand, not in his own strength, but in the strength of Christ, and it is a great help for him to see that the one in whom he is to trust has all power in heaven and in earth.

One can also use to advantage I Peter 1:5:

> "Who are kept by the power of God through faith unto salvation ready to be revealed in the last time."

and I Cor. 15:1–4. The latter passage brings out clearly the thought that the doctrine that Christ died for our sins, as blessed as it is, is not the whole Gospel, but only half of it; that the rest of the Gospel is that He was buried and that He rose again. Always get an inquirer to believe not only in Christ crucified, but in Christ risen as well. A man once came to me in deep distress of soul. He was a perfect stranger to me, but told me that he had come quite a distance to tell me his story. He said, "When I was a boy seven years of age, I started to read the Bible through. I had not gotten through Deuteronomy before I found that if one kept the whole law of God for one hundred years, and then broke it at one point, he was under the curse of a broken law. Was that right?" "Yes," I replied, "that is substantially the teaching of the law." He then continued, that he was in deep distress of soul for about a year, but as a boy of eight, he read John 3:16 and saw how Jesus Christ had died in his place, and borne the curse of the broken law for him, and he added, "My burden rolled away, and I had great joy. Was I converted?" I replied that that sounded very much like an evangelical conversion. "Well," he said, "let me tell you the rest of my story. Years passed by; I came to Chicago to live; I worked in the stockyards and lived in the stockyards region among many godless men; I fell into drink and I cannot break away; every little while this sin gets the mastery of me, and what I have come to ask you is, is there any way in which I can get the victory over sin?" I ı eplied, "There is. I am glad you have come to me; let me show you the way." I opened my Bible to I Cor. 15:1-4, and had him read:

"Moreover, brethren, I declare unto you the gospel which I preached unto you, which also ye have received, and wherein ye stand; by which also ye are saved, if ye keep in memory what I preached unto you, unless ye have believed in vain. For I delivered unto you first of all that which I also received, how that *Christ died for our sins* according to the Scriptures; and that he was buried, *and that he rose again* the third day according to the Scriptures."

Then I said to him, "What is the Gospel that Paul preached?" He answered, "That Christ died for our sins according to the Scriptures, was buried, and rose again." "That is right," I said. Then I said, "Now you have believed the first part of this Gospel, that Christ died for your sins." "Yes." "Through believing that you have found peace." "Yes." "Well," I continued, "this is only half the Gospel. If you will really believe the other half from your heart, you will get victory over your sin. Do you believe that Jesus rose again?" "Yes, I believe everything in the Bible." "Do you believe that Jesus is to-day in the place of power at the right hand of God?" "I do." "Do you believe that He has all power in heaven and on earth?" "I do." "Do you believe that this risen Christ with all power in heaven and on earth has power to set you free from the power of your sin?" "Yes," he said slowly, "I do." "Will you ask Him to do it, and trust Him to do it right now?" "I will." We knelt in prayer. I prayed and then he followed. He asked the risen Christ to set him free from the power of sin. I asked him if he really believed He had power to do it. "Yes." "Do you believe He will do it?" "Yes, I do." We rose and parted. Some time after I received a very joyous letter from him, telling me how glad he was that he had come to see me, and how the message he had heard was just the one that he needed. There are thousands of professing Christians to-day who know Jesus as a crucified Saviour, and have found pardon and peace through believing in Him, but they have never been brought to a definite, clear faith in Jesus as a risen Saviour who can save from the power of sin.

III. Show them Jesus as Lord.

It is not enough to know Jesus as a Saviour, we must know Him as Lord also. A good verse for this purpose is Acts 2:36:

"Therefore let all the house of Israel know assuredly, that *God hath made that same Jesus,* whom ye have crucified, *both Lord and Christ.*"

When the inquirer has read the verse, ask him what God hath made Jesus, and hold him to it until he replies, "Both Lord and Christ." Then say to him, "Are you willing to accept Him as your Divine Lord, the one to whom you will surrender your heart, your every thought, and word, and act?"

Another good verse for this purpose is Rom. 10:9:

"That if thou shalt confess with thy mouth *the Lord* Jesus, and shalt believe in thine heart that God hath raised him from the dead, thou shalt be saved."

When the inquirer has read the verse, ask him what we are to confess Jesus as. He should reply, "Lord." If he does not so reply, ask him other questions until he does answer in this way. Then ask him, "Do you really believe that Jesus is Lord, that He is Lord of all, that He is rightfully the absolute Lord and Master of your life and person?" Perhaps it will be well to use Acts 10:36 as throwing additional light upon this point:

"The word which God sent unto the children of Israel, preaching peace by Jesus Christ: *(he is Lord of all).*"

IV. Show them how to make Jesus their own.

It is not enough to see that Jesus is a sin-bearer, and that Jesus is a risen Saviour, and that Jesus is Lord; one must also see how to make this Jesus their own sin-bearer, their own risen Saviour, and their own Lord. There is perhaps no better verse to use for this purpose than John 1:12:

"But *as many as received him,* to them gave he power to become the sons of God, even to them that believe on his name."

When one has read the verse, you can ask to whom it is Jesus gave power to become the sons of God. "As many as received Him." "Received Him as what?" Then make it clear from what you have already said under the preceding points, that it is to receive Him as sin-bearer, to receive Him as a risen Saviour, to receive Him as our Lord and Master. "Will you just take Him as your sin-bearer now, as your risen Saviour, as your Lord and Master? Will you take Him to be whatever He offers Himself to you to be?" "I will." "Then

what does this verse show you that you have a right to call yourself?" "A son of God." "Are you a son of God?" Oftentimes the inquirer will hesitate, but go over it again and again until it is as
clear as day to him.

Another excellent passage to use for this purpose is John 3:16:

> "For God so loved the world, that he gave his only begotten Son, that
> *whosoever believeth in him* should not perish, but have everlasting life."

Ask the inquirer who it is that receives eternal life. "Whosoever
believes in Him." "Do you believe in Him as your sin-bearer?" "Do
you believe in Him as your risen Saviour?" "Do you believe in
Him as your Lord?" "Well, then, what have you?"

Another good passage to use is Acts 10:43:

> "To him give all the prophets witness, that through his name *whosoever
> believeth in him* shall receive remission of sins."

Still another is Acts 13:39:

> "And by him *all that believe* are justified from all things, from which ye
> could not be justified by the law of Moses."

V. Show the need of confessing Christ with the mouth.

No conversion is clear and satisfactory until one has been led
to confess Christ with the mouth before men. Perhaps the best
passage to show the need of such open confession with the mouth
is Rom. 10:9, 10:

> "That if thou shalt confess with thy mouth the Lord Jesus, and shalt
> believe in thine heart that God hath raised him from the dead, thou shalt
> be saved. For with the heart man believeth unto righteousness; and with
> the mouth confession is made unto salvation."

When the inquirer has read it, ask him what is the first thing this
verse tells us that we must do if we are to be saved. "Confess with
thy mouth the Lord Jesus." "Well, will you confess Jesus as your
Lord with the mouth now?" Wherever possible, it is good to get
the persons dealt with to make a public confession of Jesus just as
soon as possible. If you are dealing with them in an after-meeting,
have them make this confession right then and there; if somewhere else, bring them to a prayer-meeting, or some other service
where they can make the confession, as soon as possible.

VI. Lead into assurance.

It is not enough that one should be saved, one ought to have the assurance that he is saved. He ought to be brought to a place where he can say confidently and joyously, "*I know* I am saved, *I know* I have everlasting life." After an inquirer has been led to the acceptance and confession of Christ, an excellent passage to use for this purpose is John 3:36:

> "He that believeth on the Son *hath everlasting life:* and he that believeth not the Son shall not see life; but the wrath of God abideth on him."

When the inquirer has read the passage you can say, "Now this passage tells us that there is some one who has everlasting life; who is it?" "He that believeth on the Son." "What does God say in this passage that every one who believes on the Son has?" "Everlasting life." "Is it absolutely sure that every one who believes on the Son has everlasting life?" "It is; God says so." "Well, do you believe on the Son?" "Yes." "What have you then?" "Everlasting life." "Are you absolutely sure that you have everlasting life?" "Yes." "Why are you sure?" "Because God says so here." In many cases, probably in the majority of cases, it will be necessary to go over this again, and again, before the inquirer says that he is absolutely sure that he has everlasting life because he believes on the Son, but do not let him go until he is thus absolutely sure.

VII. Give directions as to how to live the Christian life.

It is not enough that a person be led to accept Christ, that is only the beginning of the Christian life, and if one is not shown how to lead the Christian life which he has thus begun, his life is likely to be largely one of failure. The reason so many Christian lives are comparative failures is because of a lack of definite and full instruction to the young convert as to how to lead the life which he has begun. The following instructions should be given to every one who has been dealt with as described above; and not only to them, but to every other class of inquirers that may be led to the acceptance of Christ by the methods described in the following pages or in any other way. You will speak to the inquirer somewhat as follows: "You have just begun the Christian life; now you wish to make a success of it. There are six very simple things to do, and it is absolutely sure that any one who does these six things will make a success of the Christian life."

1. "You will find the first of these in Matt. 10:32. Please read it very carefully:

"Whosoever therefore shall *confess me before men,* him will I confess also before my Father which is in heaven."

This verse tells us that Christ confesses before the Father those who confess Him before men. You will make a success of the Christian life only if Christ confesses you before the Father, so if you wish to succeed in this life that you have begun, *you must make a constant practice of confessing Christ before men.* Improve every opportunity that you get of showing your colors, and stating that you are upon Christ's side, and of telling what the Lord hath done for your soul."

2. *"Study the Word of God regularly, and hide it in your heart."* To make this point clear, use the following passages:

"*Thy word have I hid in mine heart,* that I might not sin against thee." Ps. 119:11.
"As newborn babes, desire the sincere milk of the word, that ye may grow thereby." I Pet. 2:2.

One of the most frequent causes of failure in the Christian life is neglect of the Word of God. One can no more thrive spiritually without regular spiritual food than he can thrive physically without regular and proper physical nourishment.

3. *"Pray without ceasing."* To make this point clear, use

"Pray without ceasing." I Thess. 5:17.
"But they that wait upon the Lord shall renew their strength; they shall mount up with wings as eagles; they shall run, and not be weary; and they shall walk, and not faint." Isa. 40:31.

Have the young convert read these verses again and again and mark them in his Bible.

4. *"Surrender your will absolutely to God, and obey Him in all things."* To make this plain use Acts 5:32:

"And we are his witnesses of these things; and so is also the Holy Ghost, whom God hath given *to them that obey him.*"

Show that obedience is a matter of the will more than of the outward life, and that God gives His Holy Spirit to them that obey Him, or surrender their will absolutely to Him. Insist upon the need of this absolute surrender of the will to God.

5. *"Be a constant and generous giver."* To make the necessity of this plain to the convert, use II Cor. 9:6–8:

> "But this I say, He which soweth sparingly shall reap also sparingly; and he which soweth bountifully shall reap also bountifully. Every man according as he purposeth in his heart, so let him give; not grudgingly, or of necessity: for God loveth a cheerful giver. And God is able to make all grace abound toward you; that ye, always having all sufficiency in all things, may abound to every good work."

It is well sometimes to use Mal. 3:10 as a side light:

> "Bring ye all the tithes into the storehouse, that there may be meat in mine house, and prove me now herewith, saith the Lord of hosts, if I will not open you the windows of heaven, and pour you out a blessing, that there shall not be room enough to receive it."

Go over and over it again and again until it is fixed in the young convert's mind that if he is to enjoy the fullness of God's blessing, if God is to make all grace abound toward him, he must give to the Lord's work as the Lord prospers him, that he must be a constant and generous giver. Many young Christians make little headway in the Christian life because they are not plainly instructed on the necessity of regular, systematic and generous giving to the Lord.

6. *"Go to work for Christ and keep working for Christ."* To show the necessity of this, use Matt. 25:14–30, explaining the teaching of the parable, that it is the one who uses what he has who gets more, but the one who neglects to use what he has, loses even that.

Go over these six points again and again; write them down with the texts, and give them to the young convert to take with him. The directions given above may seem to be very full, and it may occur to the reader that it will take a long time to follow them out. This is true, and oftentimes it will not be necessary to use all the texts, but at the same time it is best to be sure that you do thorough work. There is a great deal of superficial and shoddy work done in soul-winning to-day, and this kind of work does not stand. It is better to spend an hour, or two hours, on one person, and get him really rooted and grounded in the truth, than it is to get a dozen or more to say that they accept Christ, when they do not really understand what they are doing. One of the most common and greatest of faults in Christian work today is superficial dealing with souls.

CHAPTER VI

HOW TO DEAL WITH THOSE WHO HAVE
LITTLE OR NO CONCERN
ABOUT THEIR SOULS

The largest class of men and women are those who have little
or no concern about their salvation. There are some who contend
that there is no use dealing with such, but there is. It is our business when a man has no concern about his salvation to go to work
to produce that concern. How shall we do it?

I. Show him that he is a great sinner before God.

There is no better verse for this purpose than Matt. 22:37, 38:

"Jesus said unto him, Thou shalt love the Lord thy God with all thy
heart, and with all thy soul, and with all thy mind. *This is the first and
great commandment.*"

Before the one with whom you are dealing reads these verses, you
can say to him, "Do you know that you are a great sinner before
God?" Very likely he will reply, "I suppose I am a sinner, but I do
not know that I am such a great sinner." "Do you know that you
have committed the greatest sin that a man can possibly commit?"
"No, I certainly have not." "What do you think is the greatest sin
that a man can commit?" Probably he will answer, "Murder."
"You are greatly mistaken. Let us see what God says about it." Then
have him read the passage. When he has read it, ask him, "What is
the first and great commandment?" "Thou shalt love the Lord thy
God with all thy heart, and with all thy soul, and with all thy
mind." "Which commandment is this?" "The first and great commandment." "If this is the first and great commandment, what is
the first and great sin?" "Not to keep this commandment." "Have

44

you kept it? Have you put God first in everything, first in your affections, first in your thoughts, first in your pleasures, first in your business, first in everything?" "No, I have not." "What commandment, then, have you broken?" "The first and great commandment."

Some time ago a young man came into our inquiry meeting. I asked him if he was a Christian, and he replied that he was not. I asked him if he would like to be, and he said that he would. I said, "Why, then, do you not become a Christian to-night?" He replied, "I have no special interest in the matter." I said, "Do you mean that you have no conviction of sin?" "Yes," he said, "I have no conviction of sin, and am not much concerned about the whole matter." I said, "I hold in my hand a book which God has given us for the purpose of producing conviction of sin; would you like to have me use it upon you?" Half laughing, he replied, "Yes." When he had taken a seat, I had him read Matt. 22:37, 38. When he had read the passage I said to him, "What is the first and great commandment?" He read it from the Bible. I said, "If this is the first and great commandment, what is the first and great sin?" He replied, "Not to keep this commandment." I asked, "Have you kept it?" "I have not." "What have you done then?" Said he, "I have broken the first and greatest of God's commandments," and broken down with a sense of sin, then and there he went down before God and asked Him for mercy, and accepted Christ as his Saviour.

Another excellent passage to use to produce conviction of sin is Rom. 14:12:

"So then every one of us shall give account of himself to God."

The great object in using this passage is to bring the careless man face to face with God, and make him realize that he must give account to God. When he has read it, ask him, "Who has to give account?" "Every one of us." "Whom does that take in?" "Me." "Who then is to give account?" "I am." "To whom are you to give account?" "To God." "Of what are you to give account?" "Of myself." "Read it that way." "I shall give account of myself to God." "Now just let that thought sink into your heart. Say it over to yourself again and again, 'I am to give account of myself to God. I am to give account of myself to God.' Are you ready to do it?"

Amos 4:12 can be used in much the same way:

"Therefore thus will I do unto thee, O Israel: and because I will do this unto thee, *prepare to meet thy God,* O Israel."

Another very effective passage with many a careless man is Rom. 2:16:

"In the day when *God shall judge the secrets* of men by Jesus Christ according to my gospel."

When the one with whom you are dealing has read the verse, say, "What is God going to do in some coming day?" "Judge the secrets of men." "Judge what?" "The secrets of men." "Who is it that is going to judge the secrets of men?" "It is God." "Are you ready to have the secret hidden things of your life judged by a holy God?"

II. Show him the awful consequences of sin.

A very effective passage for this purpose is Rom. 6:23:

"For the wages of sin is death; but the gift of God is eternal life through Jesus Christ our Lord."

When he has read the passage, ask him, "What is the wages of sin?" "Death." Explain to him the meaning of death, literal death, spiritual death, eternal death. Now say, "This is the wages of sin; have you earned these wages?" "Are you willing to take them?" "No." "Well, there is one alternative; read the remainder of the verse." "The gift of God is eternal life through Jesus Christ our Lord." "Now you have your choice between the two, the wages that you have earned by sin, and the gift of God; which will you choose?"

Another very useful passage along this line is Is. 57:21:

"There is no peace, saith my God, to the wicked."

Another verse declaring the fearful consequences of sin, is Jno. 8:34:

"Jesus answered them, Verily, verily, I say unto you, Whosoever committeth sin is the servant of sin."

Have the one with whom you are dealing read the passage, then ask him what every one who commits sin is. "The servant of sin." "What kind of a service is that?" Bring it out that it is very degrading. Ask the inquirer if he appreciates that this is true of him, that he is the servant of sin, and then ask him if he does not want to be set free from this awful bondage.

There is another passage that one can use in much the same way, Rom. 6:16:

> "Know ye not, that to whom ye yield yourselves servants to obey, his servants ye are whom ye obey; whether of sin unto death, or of obedience unto righteousness?"

III. Show him the awfulness of unbelief in Jesus Christ.

Very few out of Christ realize that unbelief in Jesus Christ is anything very bad. Of course they know it is not just right, but that it is something awful and appalling they do not dream for a moment. They should be shown that there is nothing more appalling than unbelief in Jesus Christ. A good passage for this purpose is Jno. 3:18, 19:

> "He that believeth on him is not condemned: but he that believeth not is condemned already, because he hath not believed in the name of the only begotten Son of God. And this is the condemnation, that light is come into the world, and men loved darkness rather than light, because their deeds were evil."

When the passage has been read, say, "Now this verse tells us of some one who is condemned already; who is it?" "He that believeth not." "Believeth not on whom?" "On Jesus." "How many that believe not on Jesus are condemned already?" "Every one." "Why is every one that believeth not on Jesus condemned already?" "Because he has not believed on the name of the only begotten Son of God." "Why is this such an awful thing in the sight of God?" "Because light is come into the world, and men loved darkness rather than light because their deeds are evil." "In whom did the light come into the world?" "In Jesus." "Jesus, then, is the incarnation of light, God's fullest revelation to man: to reject Jesus, then, is the deliberate rejection of what?" "Light." "The choice of what?" "Darkness." "In rejecting Jesus, what are you rejecting?" "Light." "And what are you choosing?" "Darkness rather than light." Ask all the questions that are necessary to impress this truth upon the mind of the unbeliever, that he is deliberately rejecting the light of God, and choosing darkness rather than light.

Another very useful passage for the same purpose is Acts 2: 36, 37:

"Therefore let all the house of Israel know assuredly, that God hath made that same Jesus, whom ye have crucified, both Lord and Christ. Now when they heard this, they were pricked in their heart, and said unto Peter and to the rest of the apostles, Men and brethren, what shall we do?"

When the passage is read, say, "Now here were certain men under deep conviction of sin, crying out, 'Men and brethren, what shall we do?' What was the sin that they committed that produced such deep conviction?" "They had crucified Jesus." "What had God done with Jesus?" "He had made Him both Lord and Christ." "These men had rejected One whom God hath made both Lord and Christ. Is that a serious sin?" "Yes." "And are you not guilty of that very sin to-day? You are rejecting Jesus, and this Jesus whom you are rejecting is the very one whom God hath made both Lord and Christ. Is it not an awful sin to deliberately reject one whom God hath thus exalted?"

Another good passage to use is Jno. 16:8, 9:

"And when he is come, he will reprove the world of sin, and of righteousness, and of judgment: of sin, because they believe not on me."

When the passage has been read, ask the one with whom you are dealing, "Of what sin is it that the Holy Ghost, who knows the mind of God, especially convicts men?" "Of the sin of unbelief." "What, then, is the crowning sin in God's sight?" "Unbelief in Jesus Christ." "Why is unbelief in Jesus Christ the crowning sin in God's sight?" Then bring out that it is because it reveals most clearly the heart's deliberate choice of sin rather than righteousness, of darkness rather than light, of hatred to God rather than love to God.

In some cases it is well to use Heb. 10:28, 29:

"He that despised Moses' law died without mercy under two or three witnesses: of how much sorer punishment, suppose ye, shall he be thought worthy, who hath trodden under foot the Son of God, and hath counted the blood of the covenant, wherewith he was sanctified, an unholy thing, and hath done despite unto the Spirit of grace?"

When the passage has been read, ask the inquirer, "How serious an offense was it in God's sight to despise Moses' law?" "The one who did it died without mercy." "Is there any offense more serious in God's sight than despising the law of Moses?" "Yes, treading under foot the Son of God." "Does not every one who rejects Jesus

Christ practically tread under foot the Son of God, and count the blood of the covenant wherewith He was sanctified an unholy thing?" "Yes, I suppose he does." "Are you not committing this very sin?"

IV. Show him the awful consequences of unbelief.

For this purpose begin by using Heb. 11:6, the first of the verse:

"But without faith it is impossible to please him."

"Now this verse tells you that there is one thing that God absolutely requires if we are to please Him: what is it?" "Faith." "And no matter what else we do, if we have not faith, what is impossible for us?" "To please Him."

Follow this up by Jno. 8:24:

"I said therefore unto you, that ye shall die in your sins: for if ye believe not that I am he, ye shall die in your sins."

"What does this verse tell us will happen to you if you do not believe in Jesus?" "I shall die in my sins." Then have the inquirer read verse 21,

"Then said Jesus again unto them, I go my way, and ye shall seek me, and shall die in your sins: whither I go, ye cannot come."

That will show the result of once dying in his sins.

Further follow this up by II Thess. 1:7–9:

"And to you who are troubled rest with us, when the Lord Jesus shall be revealed from heaven with his mighty angels, in flaming fire taking vengeance on them that know not God, and that obey not the gospel of our Lord Jesus Christ: who shall be punished with everlasting destruction from the presence of the Lord, and from the glory of his power."

Say to the inquirer, "This verse tells us of a coming day in which Jesus is to take vengeance upon a certain class of people, and they are to be punished with everlasting destruction from the presence of the Lord and the glory of His power. Who is it that are to be thus punished?" "They that know not God, and that obey not the Gospel of our Lord Jesus Christ." "Are you obeying the Gospel of the Lord Jesus Christ." "No." "If, then, Christ should come now what would be your destiny?" "I should be punished with ever-lasting destruction from the presence of the Lord, and the glory of His power."

Then turn to Rev. 21:8. This verse needs no comment, it tells its own story:

> "But the fearful, and unbelieving, and the abominable, and murderers, and whoremongers, and sorcerers, and idolaters, and all liars, shall have their part in the lake which burneth with fire and brimstone: which is the second death."

Rev. 20:15 may also be used:

> "And whosoever was not found written in the book of life was cast into the lake of fire."

V. Show him that all one has to do to be lost is simply to neglect the salvation that is offered in Christ.

A verse which will serve for this purpose is Heb. 2:3:

> "How shall we escape, if we neglect so great salvation; which at the first began to be spoken by the Lord, and was confirmed unto us by them that heard him?"

When the verse has been read, ask, "What does this verse tell us is all that is necessary to be done in order to be lost?" "Simply neglect the great salvation." "That is the very thing that you are doing to-day; you are already lost. God has provided salvation for you at great cost: all you need to do to be saved, is to accept the salvation, but you cannot be saved any other way; and all you need to do to be lost, is simply to neglect it. You do not need to plunge into desperate vices, you do not need to be an open and avowed infidel, you do not need to refuse even to accept salvation, if you simply neglect it, you will be lost forever. Will you not let the question of the text sink deep into your heart: 'How shall we escape if we neglect so great salvation?'"

Another passage to use for this purpose is Acts 3:22, 23:

> "For Moses truly said unto the fathers, A prophet shall the Lord your God raise up unto you of your brethren, like unto me; him shall ye hear in all things whatsoever he shall say unto you. And it shall come to pass that every soul, which will not hear that prophet, shall be destroyed from among the people."

"This passage tells us about a Prophet that Moses said the Lord would raise up. Who was that Prophet?" "Jesus." "What does God tell us to do with that Prophet?" "Hear him 'in all things whatsoever he shall say unto you.'" "What shall happen unto him who does not hearken unto the words of that Prophet?" "He shall be destroyed from among the people." "Are you hearkening unto the words of that Prophet?"

Still another passage to use is Acts 13:38–41:

> "Be it known unto you therefore, men and brethren, that through this man is preached unto you the forgiveness of sins: and by him all that believe are justified from all things, from which ye could not be justified by the law of Moses.
> "Beware therefore, lest that come upon you, which is spoken of in the prophets; Behold, ye despisers, and wonder, and perish: for I work a work in your days, a work which ye shall in no wise believe, though a man declare it unto you."

"These verses tell us about Jesus. They tell us of something that is preached to us through Him. What is it?" "Forgiveness of sins." "They tell us what it is that a man has to do to obtain this forgiveness of sins; what is it?" "Believe on Him." "What blessing comes to all that believe?" "They are justified from all things." "On the other hand, what comes to us if we neglect to believe?" "We shall perish."

Still another passage to use for this purpose is Jno. 3:36:

> "He that believeth on the Son hath everlasting life: and he that believeth not the Son shall not see life; but the wrath of God abideth on him."

When the passage has been read, ask, "What does every one who believes on the Son get?" "Everlasting life." "But on the other hand, if one simply neglects to believe what will be the result?" "He shall not see life, but the wrath of God abideth upon him."

VI. Show him the wonderful love of God to him.

Oftentimes when every other method of dealing with the careless fails, a realization of the love of God breaks the heart, and leads to an acceptance of Christ. There is no better passage to show the love of God than Jno. 3:16:

> "For God so loved the world, that he gave his only begotten Son, that whosoever believeth in him should not perish, but have everlasting life."

Generally it will need no comment. I was once dealing with one of the most careless and vile women I ever met. She moved in good society, but in her secret life was as vile as a woman of the street. She told me the story of her life in a most shameless and unblushing way, half-laughing as she did it. I made no further reply than to ask her to read Jno. 3:16 to which I had opened my Bible. Before she had read the passage through, she burst into tears, her heart broken by the love of God to her.

Another excellent passage to use in the same way is Is. 53:5:

> "But he was wounded for our transgressions, he was bruised for our iniquities; the chastisement of our peace was upon him; and with his stripes we are healed."

God used this passage one night to bring to tears and penitence one of the most stubborn and wayward young women with whom I ever dealt. I made almost no comment, simply read the passage to her. The Spirit of God seemed to hold up before her, her Saviour, wounded for her transgressions, and bruised for her iniquities. Her stubborn will gave way, and before many days she was rejoicing in Christ.

Two other passages which can be used in the same way are Gal. 3:13 and I Pet. 2:24:

> "Christ hath redeemed us from the curse of the law, being made a curse for us: for it is written, Cursed is every one that hangeth on a tree:"
> "Who his own self bare our sins in his own body on the tree, that we, being dead to sins, should live unto righteousness: by whose stripes ye were healed."

After showing the love of God through the use of such passages as these mentioned, it is oftentimes well to clinch this truth by using Rom. 2:4, 5:

> "Or despisest thou the riches of his goodness and forbearance and long-suffering; not knowing that the goodness of God leadeth thee to repentance? But after thy hardness and impenitent heart treasurest up unto thyself wrath against the day of wrath and revelation of the righteous judgment of God."

Before having the passage read, say, "We have been looking at the love of God to you; now let us see what God tells us is the purpose of that love, and what will be the result of our despising it." Then have the passage, Rom. 2:4, 5 read by the one with whom you are dealing. When he has read it, ask him what is the purpose of God's goodness. "To lead to repentance." "If it does not lead us to repentance, what does it show us about our hearts?" "That they are very hard and impenitent." "And if we refuse to let the goodness of God lead us to repentance, what will be the result?" "We treasure up wrath unto ourselves against the day of wrath and revelation of the righteous judgment of God."

Of course it will not always be possible to get a person who has little or no concern about his salvation to talk with you long enough to go over all these passages, but not infrequently he will become so interested after the use of the first or second passage that he will be glad to go through. Oftentimes it is not at all necessary to use all these passages. Not infrequently I find that the first passage, Matt. 22:37, 38, does the desired work, but it is well to be thorough, and to use all the passages necessary.

Sometimes one will not talk with you for any length of time at all. In such a case, the best thing to do is to select a very pointed and searching passage and give it to him, repeating it again and again, and then as he goes, say to him something like this, "I am going to ask God to burn that passage into your heart"; and then do not forget to do what you said you were going to do. Good passages for this purpose are Rom. 6:23; Mark 16:16; Jno. 3:36; Is. 57:21.

When the inquirer has been led by the use of any or all of these passages to realize his need of a Saviour, and really desires to be saved, of course he comes under the class treated in the preceding chapter, and should be dealt with accordingly. It is not intended that the worker shall follow the precise method laid down here, which is given rather by way of suggestion, but the general plan here outlined has been honored of God to the salvation of very many. But let us be sure, whether we use this method or some other, to do thoroughgoing and lasting work.

Of course it is not supposed that the inquirer will always answer you exactly as stated above. If he does not, make use of the answers that he does give, or if necessary ask the same question another way until he does answer you correctly. The answers given to the questions are found in the text, but people have a great habit of not seeing what is plainly stated in a Scripture text. Oftentimes when they do not answer right, it is well to ask them to look at the verse again, and repeat the question, and keep asking questions until they do give the right answer. Perhaps the inquirer will try to switch you off on to some sidetrack. Do not permit him to do this, but hold right to the matter in hand.

CHAPTER VII

HOW TO DEAL WITH THOSE
WHO HAVE DIFFICULTIES

We will find that a very large number of the persons whom we try to lead to Christ are really anxious to be saved, and know how, but are confronted with difficulties which they deem important or even insurmountable. Whenever it is possible, it is well to show such persons their need of Christ before taking up a specific difficulty. In this way many of the supposed difficulties are dissipated. Oftentimes even when people really are anxious to be saved, there is not that deep, clear, and intelligent knowledge of their need of Christ that is desirable. It is usually a waste of time to take up specific difficulties until there is this clear and definite sense of need.

I. "I am too great a sinner."

This is a difficulty that is very real, and very often met, but fortunately it is also one with which it is very easy to deal. The method of treatment is as follows:

1. *General treatment.* There is no better passage to use to meet this difficulty than I Tim. 1:15:

"This is a faithful saying, and worthy of all acceptation, that Christ Jesus came into the world *to save sinners; of whom I am chief."*

This verse so exactly fits the case, that there is little need for comment. At the close of a Sunday morning service, I spoke to a man of intelligence and ability, but who had gone down into the deepest depth of sin. When asked why he was not a Christian, he replied, "I am too great a sinner to be saved." I turned him at once to I Tim. 1:15. No sooner had I read the verse than he replied,

"Well, I am the chief of sinners." "That verse means you, then." He replied, "It is a precious promise." I said, "Will you accept it now?" "I will." Then I said, "Let us kneel down and tell God so." We knelt down and he confessed to God his sins, and asked God for Christ's sake to forgive him. When he had finished his prayer, I asked him if he really had accepted Christ, and he said that he had. I asked him if he really believed that he was accepted, and he said he did. He took the first opportunity afforded him of confessing Christ, and became an active Christian. His broken home was restored, and every day he was found witnessing for his Master.

Another useful passage in dealing with this class is Matt. 9: 12, 13:

> "But when Jesus heard that, he said unto them, They that be whole need not a physician, but they that are sick. But go ye and learn what that meaneth, I will have mercy, and not sacrifice; for I am not come to call the righteous, but sinners to repentance."

This shows the inquirer at once that his sin, instead of being an obstacle in the way of his coming to Christ, really fits him for coming to Christ, as He has not come to call the righteous, but sinners to repentance.

I have frequently used Rom. 5:6–8:

> "For when we were yet without strength, in due time Christ died for the ungodly. For scarcely for a righteous man will one die: yet peradventure for a good man some would even dare to die. But God commendeth his love towards us, in that, while we were yet sinners, Christ died for us."

At the close of an evening service in Minneapolis, a man who had raised his hand for prayer, hurried away as soon as the benediction was pronounced. I hastened after him, laid my hand upon his shoulder, and said, "Did you not hold your hand up to-night for prayer?" "Yes." "Why then are you hurrying away?" He replied, "There is no use talking to me." I said, "God loves you." He replied, "You do not know whom you are talking to." "I do not care whom I am talking to, but I know God loves you." He said, "I am the meanest thief in Minneapolis." "Then I know God loves you"; and I opened my Bible to Rom. 5:6–8 and read the passage through. "Now," I said, "if you are the meanest thief in Minneapolis, you are a sinner, and this verse tells us that God loves sinners." The Spirit of God carried the message of love home to his heart, he broke down, and going with me into another room, he told me the story of his life. He had been released from confinement that day, and had started out that night to commit what he said would have been one of the most daring burglaries ever committed in Minneapolis. With his two companions in crime, he was passing a corner where we were holding an open-air meeting. He stopped a few moments to hear what was going on, and in spite of the oaths and protests of his companions, stayed through the meeting, and went with us into the mission. It so happened that a few days before he had dreamed in confinement of his mother, and the hearing of the Gospel added to this, and the few words that had been spoken to him personally, had completed the work. After he had told me his story, we knelt in prayer. Utterly overcome with emotion, through falling tears he looked to God for pardon, and left the room rejoicing in the assurance that his sins had all been forgiven.

It is often well to say to the man who thinks that he is too great a sinner, "Your sins are great, greater far than you think, but they are all settled." In order to show him how they are settled, and to make it clear that they are settled, turn to Is. 53:6:

2. *Special cases.* Among those who regard themselves as too great sinners to be saved, there are special cases:

(1) *The man who says, "I am lost."*

If the difficulty is stated in this way, it is well to use Luke 19: 10, as that fits so exactly the inquirer's statement of the case; for the verse says:

"For the Son of man is come to seek and to save *that which was lost.*"

I was once speaking to a young man who was the complete sla of drink and other sins, and urging him to accept the Saviour. H turned to me in a despairing way and said, "Mr. Torrey, go talk to those other men, there is no use talking to me, I am lost." I replied, "If you are lost, I have a message from God's Word addressed directly to you." I turned to Luke 19:10 and read, "For the Son of man is come to seek and to save that which was lost." The text fitted the case so exactly, that there was no need of comment or explanation on my part.

(2) *Murderers.*

Among those who think that they are too great sinners to be saved, murderers form an especial class. I find that not a few who have stained their hands with the blood of a fellow-man have a deep-seated impression that there is no hope for a man who has committed this sin. Is. 1:18 is very useful in such a case. One night I was dealing with a man who was sure that he was beyond all hope. I asked him why he thought so, and he replied, because he had taken the life of a fellow man. I said, "Let me read you something from God's Word, and I read:

> "Come now, and let us reason together, saith the Lord: though your sins be as scarlet, they shall be as white as snow; though they be red like crimson, they shall be as wool."

I said, "If you have taken the life of a fellow man, your sins are as scarlet." "Oh," he cried, "the bullet was scarlet, I can see it now." Then I asked him to listen again to the promise, "Though your sins be as scarlet, they shall be as white as snow; though they be red like crimson, they shall be as wool." He saw how the promise exactly covered his case, and it brought hope into a heart that had been filled with despair.

Another useful passage is Ps. 51:14:

> "Deliver me from bloodguiltiness, O God, thou God of my salvation."

In using this passage, I always call the inquirer's attention to the fact that it is the prayer of a man who had himself stained his hands with the blood of a fellow man. Then I tell him how God heard the prayer, and delivered him from bloodguiltiness, and then turn to Ps. 32:5 containing the Psalmist's own statement as to how his sin of bloodguiltiness was forgiven.

> "I acknowledged my sin unto thee, and mine iniquity have I not hid. I said, I will confess my transgressions unto the Lord; and thou forgavest the iniquity of mv sin."

3. *General remarks.*

(1) *Never give false comfort by telling the inquirer, "You are not a very great sinner."*

This mistake is often made. Tenderhearted people are greatly disturbed over the deep conviction of sin that the Spirit of God produces in the hearts of men, and try to give comfort by telling the inquirer that he is not so great a sinner after all. This is false comfort. There is no man but who is a greater sinner than he ever thinks or realizes.

(2) After meeting the specific difficulty, show the inquirer how to be saved. The method of doing this is explained in Chapter V. This remark applies not only to this difficulty, but to all the difficulties that follow. It is not enough to remove difficulties, we must bring inquirers to a saving knowledge of Christ.

II. "My heart is too hard."

One of the passages given under the former difficulty will also be useful here, Luke 19:10. Before using it, it may be well to say, "Well, then, if your heart is so hard and wicked, you must be lost." "Yes, I am lost." "Very well, I have a promise for you." Turn to Luke 19:10 and let them read. "You said that your heart was so hard and wicked that you were lost." "Yes." "And this verse tells us that Jesus Christ is come to seek and to save whom?" "The lost." "And that means you. Will you let Him save you now?"

Another useful passage is Jno. 6:37, the last half of the verse,

"Him that cometh to me I will in no wise cast out."

You can say, "You think your heart is so hard and wicked that you cannot be saved, but would you be willing to come to Christ if He would accept you?" "Yes." "Well, let us listen to what He says." Then read the passage, "Him that cometh to me I will in no wise cast out." "Whom does Jesus say here that He will receive?" "Any one who comes." "Does He say He will receive any one who comes provided his heart is not too hard and wicked?" "No." "What does He say?" "That He will receive any one who comes." "Then He will receive any one who comes no matter how hard and wicked their heart?" "Yes." "Will you come now?"

Ez. 36:26, 27 is helpful in many cases. You can say to the inquirer, "Yes, your heart is too hard and wicked, but let us see what God promises to do." Then have him read the passage:

"A new heart also will I give you, and a new spirit will I put within you: and I will take away the stony heart out of your flesh, and I will give you an heart of flesh. And I will put my spirit within you, and cause you to walk in my statutes, and ye shall keep my judgments, and do them."

"What does God here promise to give?" "A new heart." "Are you willing that He should give you a new heart in place of that hard and wicked heart that you have?"

Another passage which is helpful in much the same way is II Cor. 5:17:

"Therefore if any man be in Christ, he is a new creature: old things are passed away; behold, all things are become new."

"Yes," you can say to the one in trouble, "your heart is too hard and wicked. What you need is to be made all over new; there is a way to be made all over, to get a new heart and to be a new man. Let me show you what that way is." Then let him read the passage. When he has read it, ask him, "What does the one who accepts Christ become?" "A new creature." "What becomes of the old things?" "They are passed away." "Do you want to be a new creature, and have old things pass away?" "Yes." "What then is all that you have to do?" "Accept Christ." "Will you do it?"

III. "I must become better before I become a Christian."

This is a very real difficulty with many people. They sincerely believe that they cannot come to Christ just as they are in their sins, that they must do something to make themselves better before they can come to Him. You can show them that they are utterly mistaken in this by having them read Matt. 9:12, 13:

"But when Jesus heard that, he said unto them, They that be whole need not a physician, but they that are sick. But go ye and learn what that meaneth, I will have mercy and not sacrifice: for I am not come to call the righteous, but sinners to repentance."

When they have read it, if they do not see the point for themselves, you can ask, "To what does Jesus compare Himself in this verse?" "To a physician." "Who is it needs a physician, well people or sick people?" "Sick people." "Ought a person who is sick to wait until he gets well before he gets the doctor?" "No, of course not." "Ought a person who is spiritually sick to wait until he is better before he comes to Jesus?" "No." "Who is it Jesus invites to come to Himself, good people or bad people?" "Bad people." "Is then the fact that you are not good a reason for waiting or a reason for coming to Jesus at once?"

Luke 15:18–24 also fits the case exactly. Show the inquirer that we have in this story a picture of God's relation to the sinner, that God wishes us to understand that He would have the sinner come in all his rags, and that He will give him a hearty welcome, a robe, a ring and a feast if he comes just as he is.

Luke 18:10–14 also applies. You can say, "Here are two men who came to God. One came on the ground that he was a sinner, the other came on the ground that he was righteous. Which of the two did God accept?" "The one who came on the ground that he was a sinner." "Well, God would have you come just the same way."

IV. "I cannot hold out," (or "I am afraid I shall fail if I try").

1. *General treatment.* First see if the inquirer is in dead earnest, and if there is not some other difficulty lying back of this. Many a man gives this as a difficulty, when perhaps it is not the real one.

There is perhaps no better verse in the Bible for this difficulty than Jude 24:

"Now unto him that is *able to keep you from falling,* and to present you faultless before the presence of his glory with exceeding joy."

Its application is so plain as to need no comment.

Another useful passage is I Pet. 1:5:

"Who are *kept by the power of God* through faith unto salvation ready to be revealed in the last time."

When the inquirer has read it, ask him by whose power it is that we are kept. Then you can say, "It is not then a question of our strength at all, but of God's strength. Do you think that God is able to keep you?"

Other passages which are helpful along the same line are:

"For the which cause I also suffer these things: nevertheless I am not ashamed: for I know whom I have believed, and am persuaded that *he is able to keep* that which I have committed unto him against that day." II Tim. 1:12.

"Fear thou not; for I am with thee: be not dismayed; for I am thy God: I will strengthen thee; yea, I will help thee; yea, I will uphold thee with the right hand of my righteousness." Is. 41:10.

"For I the Lord thy God will hold thy right hand, saying unto thee, Fear not; I will help thee." Is. 41:13.

A passage which will help by showing the absolute security of Christ's sheep, is Jno. 10:28, 29:

"And I give unto them eternal life; and they shall never perish, neither shall any man pluck them out of my hand. My Father, which gave them me, is greater than all; and no man is able to pluck them out of my Father's hand."

In many cases a good passage to use is Heb. 7:25:

"Wherefore he is able also to save them to the uttermost that come unto God by him, seeing he ever liveth to make intercession for them."

2. *Special cases.*

(1) *Those afraid of some temptation that will prove too strong.* The best passage to use in such a case is I Cor. 10:13:

"There hath no temptation taken you but such as is common to man; but God is faithful, who will not suffer you to be tempted above that ye are able; but will with the temptation also make a way to escape, that ye may be able to bear it."

(2) *Those who dwell upon their own weakness.*

"And he said unto me, My grace is sufficient for thee; for *my strength is made perfect in weakness.* Most gladly therefore will I rather glory in my infirmities that the power of Christ may rest upon me." II Cor. 12:9, 10.

"He giveth power to the faint; and to them that have no might he increaseth strength. Even the youths shall faint and be weary, and the young men shall utterly fall: but they that wait upon the Lord shall renew their strength; they shall mount up with wings as eagles; they shall run, and not be weary; and they shall walk, and not faint." Is. 40:29–31.

One evening a lady called me to a man whom she was trying to lead to Christ and asked me if I could help him. I said to him, "What is your difficulty?" He replied, "I have no strength." "Ah," I said, "I have a message that exactly fits your case," and read Is.

40:29, "He giveth power to the faint, and to them that have no might he increaseth strength." "You say you have no strength, that is, no might; now this verse tells us that to those who have no might, that is to people just like you, God increaseth strength." The Holy Spirit took the word of comfort home to his heart at once, and he put his trust in Jesus Christ then and there.

V. "I cannot give up my evil ways."

1. *You must or perish.* In order to prove this statement, use:

"For the wages of sin is death; but the gift of God is eternal life through Jesus Christ our Lord." Rom. 6:23.

"Be not deceived; God is not mocked: for whatsoever a man soweth, that shall he also reap. For he that soweth to his flesh shall of the flesh reap corruption; but he that soweth to the Spirit shall of the Spirit reap life everlasting." Gal. 6:7, 8.

"But the fearful, and unbelieving, and the abominable, and murderers, and whoremongers, and sorcerers, and idolaters, and all liars, shall have their part in the lake which burneth with fire and brimstone: which is the second death." Rev. 21.8.

Drive this thought home. Show the inquirer no quarter, but keep ringing the changes on the thought, "You must give up your evil ways or perish." Emphasize it by Scripture. When the inquirer sees and realizes this, then you can pass on to the next thought.

2. *You can in the strength of Jesus Christ.* To prove this, have the inquirer read Phil. 4:13, and Jno. 8:36:

"I can do all things through Christ which strengtheneth me."
"If the Son therefore shall make you free, ye shall be free indeed."

3. *Show the risen Christ with all power in heaven and on earth.* It is in the power of the risen Christ, and through union with Him, that we are enabled to give up our evil ways, so the one who has this difficulty should have the fact that Christ is risen made clear to him. The following passages will serve well for this purpose.

"Moreover, brethren, I declare unto you the Gospel which I preached unto you, which also ye have received, and wherein ye stand; by which also ye are saved, if ye keep in memory what I preached unto you, unless ye have believed in vain. For I delivered unto you first of all that which I also received, how that Christ died for our sins according to the Scriptures; and that he was buried, and that he rose again the third day according to the Scriptures." I Cor. 15:1–4.

"And Jesus came and spake unto them, saying, All power is given unto me in heaven and in earth." Matt. 28:18.

"Wherefore he is able also to save them to the uttermost that come unto God by him, seeing he ever liveth to make intercession for them." Heb. 7:25.

4. *Show how to get victory over sin.* There is perhaps nothing in the Bible that makes the way of victory over sin more plain and simple than Rom. 6:12–14:

"Let not sin therefore reign in your mortal body, that ye should obey it in the lusts thereof. Neither yield ye your members as instruments of unrighteousness unto sin: but *yield yourselves unto God,* as those that are alive from the dead, and your members as instruments of righteousness unto God. For sin shall not have dominion over you: for ye are not under the law, but under grace."

You can say to the inquirer, "In this verse we are told how to get victory over sin: we are told what not to do, and what to do. What is it we are told not to do?" "Not to let sin reign in our mortal body; not to yield our members as instruments of unrighteousness unto sin." "What are we told to do?" "To yield ourselves unto God as those that are alive from the dead; and to yield our members as instruments of righteousness unto God." "Now do you believe that through union with the risen Christ your Saviour, you are alive from the dead? Will you yield or present yourself unto God as one alive from the dead? Will you now and here present your members as instruments of righteousness unto God?" After the inquirer has been led to do this, show him that whatever we yield to God, God accepts, and that he can now TRUST God for victory over sin, and have deliverance from his evil ways.

VI. "I have tried before and failed."

Those who have tried to be Christians and have failed in the attempt, very naturally hesitate about trying again, and such a case needs to be dealt with, with great care, wisdom and thoroughness.

1. The first thing to do is to say to such a one, *"I can show you how to try and not fail."* Then point him to II Cor. 9:8:

"And God is able to make all grace abound toward you; that ye, always having all sufficiency in all things, may abound to every good work."

When the person has read the verse, to be sure that he gets its meaning you can say, "This verse tells us that God is able to make all grace abound toward us, that we, 'always having all sufficiency in all things, may abound to every good work.' It is clear then, that there is a way to try and not fail."

2. *Find out the cause of failure.* In finding out the cause of failure, there are seven points to be looked into:

(1) *Did you put all your trust for pardon in the finished work of Christ?*

This is a very frequent cause of failure in the attempt to be a Christian, the person has never been led to see clearly the ground of his salvation, and to trust wholly in the finished work of Christ for pardon. Is. 53:6 is a useful passage at this point:

"All we like sheep have gone astray; we have turned every one to his own way; and the Lord hath laid on him the iniquity of us all."

(2) *Did you surrender absolutely to God?*

Many are led to make a profession of faith in Christ without having been led to absolute surrender and the Christian life thus begun, is very likely to prove a failure. The passage to use at this point is Acts 5:32:

"And we are his witnesses of these things; and so is also the Holy Ghost, whom God hath given to them that obey him."

(3) *Did you confess Christ openly before men?*

This is one of the most frequent causes of failure. I have talked with very many who have said that they have tried to be Christians and failed, and a very large proportion of them I have found failed at this very point, the lack of a constant, open confession of Christ. Good passages to use at this point are Matt. 10:32, 33 and Rom. 10:10:

"Whosoever therefore shall confess me before men, him will I confess also before my Father which is in heaven. But whosoever shall deny me before men, him will I also deny before my Father which is in heaven."
"For with the heart man believeth unto righteousness; and with the mouth confession is made unto salvation."

(4) *Did you study the Word of God daily?*

Here is another frequent cause of failure, neglect of the Bible. Very few of those who have really begun the Christian life, and who have made a practice of daily study of the Word, fail in their attempt to be Christians. Good passages to use at this point are I Pet. 2:2 and Ps. 119:11:

"As newborn babes, desire the sincere milk of the word, that ye may grow thereby."

"Thy word have I hid in mine heart that I might not sin against thee."

(5) *Did you look each day to God alone, and not to self at all, for strength and victory?*

To emphasize this question, use:

"He giveth power to the faint; and to them that have no might he increaseth strength." Is. 40:29.

"And he said unto me, My grace is sufficient for thee; for my strength is made perfect in weakness. Most gladly therefore will I rather glory in my infirmities, that the power of Christ may rest upon me." II Cor. 12:9.

"Likewise, ye younger, submit yourselves unto the elder. Yea, all of you be subject one to another, and be clothed with humility: for God resisteth the proud, and giveth grace to the humble." I Pet. 5:5.

(6) *Did you pray constantly?*

Use at this point:

"Pray without ceasing." I Thess. 5:17.

"He giveth power to the faint; and, to them that have no might he increaseth strength. Even the youths shall faint and be weary, and the young men shall utterly fall: but *they that wait upon the Lord* shall renew their strength; they shall mount up with wings as eagles; they shall run, and not be weary; and they shall walk, and not faint." Is. 40: 29-31.

"Let us therefore come boldly unto the throne of grace, that we may obtain mercy, and find grace to help in time of need." Heb. 4:16.

(7) *Did you go to work for Christ?*

Here use Matt. 25:14-29.

VII. "The Christian life is too hard."

1. If a person states this as his difficulty, first show him that *the Christian life is not hard.* In Matt. 11:30 Christ tells us His yoke is easy:

"For my yoke is easy, and my burden is light."

Prov. 3:17 shows us that wisdom's ways are ways of pleasantness,

"Her ways are ways of pleasantness, and all her paths are peace."

I Jno. 5:3, that God's commandments are not grievous:

"For this is the love of God, that we keep his commandments; and his commandments are not grievous."

I Pet. 1:8 pictures the Christian life as a life of joy unspeakable and full of glory:

"Whom having not seen, ye love; in whom, though now ye see him not, yet believing, ye rejoice with joy unspeakable and full of glory."

In using the latter passage you might say, "We have a picture of the Christian life in I Pet. 1:8, let us see if it is a hard life." Have the inquirer read the verse, and then ask, "What kind of a life according to this passage, is the Christian life?" "A life of joy unspeakable and full of glory." "Do you think that is hard?"

2. Show him that *the way of sin is hard.* Show the inquirer that it is not the Christian life, but the life without Christ that is the hard life. For this purpose use the last half of Prov. 13:15, and Is. 57:21:

"But the way of transgressors is hard."
"There is no peace, saith my God, to the wicked."

VIII. "There is too much to give up."

This is often the difficulty even when not stated.

1. First show the inquirer that *no matter how much there may be to give up, it is better to give up anything than to lose one's soul.* For this purpose use Mark 8:36:

"For what shall it profit a man, if he shall gain the whole world, and lose his own soul?"

2. Show the inquirer that *the only things we have to give up are the things which will harm us.* This is made clear by Ps. 84:11:

"For the Lord God is a sun and shield; the Lord will give grace and glory; *no good thing will he withhold* from them that walk uprightly."

When the inquirer has read the verse, ask him, "What does this verse tell us that God will not withhold from us?" "Any good thing." "The things then that God asks you to give up, are what kind of things?" "Evil things." "Then all God asks you to give up are the things which are harmful to you. Do you wish to keep them?"

I have found Rom. 8:32 very effective, for it emphasizes the thought that if God loved us enough to give His Son to die for us on the Cross, He will freely give us all things:

"He that spared not his own Son, but delivered him up for us all, how shall he not with him also freely give us all things?"

I once had a long conversation with a young woman who was having a great struggle about accepting Christ. She was very fond of the world and certain forms of amusement, which she felt she would have to give up if she became a Christian. Finally I said to her, "Do you think God loves you?" "Yes, I know He does." "How much does God love you?" "Enough to give His Son to die for me," she replied. "Do you think if God loved you enough to give His Son to die for you, He will ask you to give up anything that is for your good to keep?" "No, certainly He will not." "Do you wish to keep anything not for your good to keep?" "No." "Then do you not think you had better accept Jesus Christ right here and now?" "Yes," and she did.

Another verse which is useful as showing the inquirer that the things which he has to give up are the things which are passing away, is I Jno. 2:15–17:

"Love not the world, neither the things that are in the world. If any man love the world, the love of the Father is not in him. For all that is in the world, the lust of the flesh, and the lust of the eyes, and the pride of life, is not of the Father, but is of the world. And *the world passeth away*, and the lust thereof: but he that doeth the will of God abideth for ever."

3. Show the inquirer that *what we give up is nothing to what we get*. For this purpose use Phil. 3:7, 8:

"But what things were gain to me, those I counted loss for Christ. Yea, doubtless, and I count all things but loss for the excellency of the knowledge of Christ Jesus my Lord; for whom I have suffered the loss of all things, and do count them but dung, that I may win Christ."

You can call the inquirer's attention to the fact that it was Paul who spoke these words, that perhaps no one ever gave up more for Christ than he did, and yet he here tells us that what he gave up was to what he got only as the refuse of the street.

4. Show the inquirer that *if he rejects Christ for fear of what he will have to give up if he accepts Him, he will make a terrible mistake.* Then you can say to him, "The Bible pictures to us a man who made this very mistake. Will you read the story of his folly and its consequences?" Then turn to Luke 12:16–21 and let the inquirer read it. When he has read it, ask him if he is willing to follow in the footsteps of the man in the passage.

IX. **"I cannot be a Christian in my business,"** (or "It will hurt my business," or "I will lose my position.")

This is a very real difficulty with many, and must be met honestly and squarely.

1. It is well to bear in mind that even when a man really thinks this is true, it is not always so. Many people have an idea that it is impossible to be a Christian in any line of business except Christian work. They must be shown that this is a mistake. When a man makes this excuse, it is often well to ask him what his business is, and why he cannot be a Christian in it. Sometimes you will find that it is a business in which there are many Christians, and you can tell him that there are many Christians in the same business.

2. But oftentimes it is true that the man with whom you are dealing is in a business in which it is impossible to be a Christian. For example, the man may be a bartender or a theatrical manager or something of that sort. In that case say to the man, "You had better lose your business (or position) than to lose your soul." To drive this statement home, use Mark 8:36:

"For what shall it profit a man, if he shall gain the whole world, and lose his own soul?"

Do not pass on to the next point until the man sees this and realizes it. Make the man feel that he had better lose every dollar that he has in the world than to lose his soul. When the man sees this, and is ready to give up his business at any cost, you can use Matt. 6:33:

> "But seek ye first the kingdom of God, and his righteousness; and all these things shall be added unto you."

This verse will show him that if he puts God and His kingdom first, all needful things will be supplied to him. It is better to starve than to reject Christ, but no man who accepts Christ will be left to starve.

Another very useful passage is Mark 10:29, 30:

> "And Jesus answered and said, Verily I say unto you, There is no man that hath left house, or brethren, or sisters, or father, or mother, or wife, or children, or lands, for my sake, and the gospel's, but he shall receive an hundred fold now in this time, houses, and brethren, and sisters, and mothers, and children, and lands, with persecutions; and in the world to come eternal life."

X. "I will lose my friends."

Many a person who contemplates beginning the Christian life has none but ungodly companions, and he sees very clearly that if he becomes a Christian he will lose these friends, the only ones that he has; so this difficulty is a very real one.

1. First show the inquirer that he is better off without these friends, for they are enemies of God. Use for this purpose James 4:4:

> "Ye adulterers and adulteresses, know ye not that the friendship of the world is enmity with God? whosoever therefore will be a friend of the world is the enemy of God."

Before giving it to the inquirer to read, say, "Yes, it may be that you will lose your friends, but if your friends are godless, you are better off without them. See what God's Word says about it." Then show him the passage. If this verse does not prove sufficiently effective, follow it up with Prov. 13:20:

> "He that walketh with wise men shall be wise: but a companion of fools shall be destroyed."

Follow this up with Ps. 1:1, 2:

> "Blessed is the man that walketh not in the counsel of the ungodly, nor standeth in the way of sinners, nor sitteth in the seat of the scornful.

But his delight is in the law of the Lord; and in his law doth he meditate day and night."

Call the inquirer's attention to the fact that God has promised an especial blessing to those who turn their backs upon godless friendships in order to obey Him.

2. Having made this first point clear, you can say, "You may lose your godless friends, but you will get better friends," and turn him to I John 1:3:

"That which we have seen and heard declare we unto you, that ye also may have fellowship with us; and truly our fellowship is with the Father, and with his Son Jesus Christ."

When they have read it you can say, "If you do lose your godless friends by coming to Christ, what two new friends do you get?" "The Father and His Son Jesus Christ." "Which would you rather have for friends, your godless worldly companions, or God the Father and His Son Jesus Christ?" All this may be followed up again by Mark 10:29, 30.

XI. "I am afraid of ridicule."

1. Show the awful peril in being governed by the fear of man. Use Prov. 29:25:

"The fear of man bringeth a snare; but whoso putteth his trust in the Lord shall be safe."

You might explain that this snare which catches him who is afraid of ridicule and rejects Christ, often results in the eternal ruin of the soul.

Next use Mark 8:38:

"Whosoever therefore shall be ashamed of me and of my words in this adulterous and sinful generation, of him also shall the Son of man be ashamed, when he cometh in the glory of his Father with the holy angels."

2. Show that it is a glorious privilege to be ridiculed for Christ. Use for this purpose Matt. 5:11, 12:

"Blessed are ye, when men shall revile you, and persecute you, and shall say all manner of evil against you falsely, for my sake. Rejoice, and be exceeding glad; for great is your reward in heaven: for so persecuted they the prophets which were before you."

XII. "I will be persecuted if I become a Christian."

Never tell any one that he will not be persecuted. On the contrary say, "Yes, I presume you will be persecuted, for God tells us in His Word, that all who live godly in Christ Jesus shall suffer persecution." To prove it show him II Tim. 3:12:

> "Yea, and all that will live godly in Christ Jesus shall suffer persecution."

But then tell him that it is a great privilege to be persecuted for Christ's sake, and brings an abundant reward. Have him read Matt. 5:10–12, and drive home the thought that we ought to rejoice at the privilege of being persecuted rather than to shrink from being a Christian on that account.

Then show him the result of suffering with Christ. Turn to II Tim. 2:12:

> "If we suffer, we shall also reign with him; if we deny him, he also will deny us."

Use Rom. 8:18 to show him how small are the sufferings of this present time in comparison with the glory that we shall obtain through them:

> "For I reckon that the sufferings of this present time are not worthy to be compared with the glory which shall be revealed in us." (Comp. II Cor. 4:17.)

Acts 5:40, 41 is useful as showing how the early church regarded persecution, rejoicing in it rather than shrinking from it:

> "And to him they agreed: and when they had called the apostles, and beaten them, they commanded that they should not speak in the name of Jesus, and let them go. And they departed from the presence of the council, rejoicing that they were counted worthy to suffer shame for his name."

Another passage which is also useful in such a case is I Pet. 2:20, 21:

> "For what glory is it, if, when ye be buffeted for your faults, ye shall take it patiently? but if, when ye do well, and suffer for it, ye take it patiently, this is acceptable with God. For even hereunto were ye called; because Christ also suffered for us, leaving us an example, that ye should follow his steps."

XIII. "I have no feeling."

This is a very common difficulty. There are many who wish to come to Christ, but do not think they can come because they have not the proper feeling. The first thing to do in such a case, is to find out what feeling the inquirer thinks it is necessary to have in order to become a Christian.

1. *"The joy and peace that Christians tell about."* The feeling that many inquirers are waiting for is the joy and peace that Christians speak of. Of course the thing to do in such a case, is to show the inquirer that this joy and peace is the result of coming to Christ, and that we cannot expect the result before we come. The first passage to use to show this is Gal. 5:22:

> "But the fruit of the Spirit is love, joy, peace, long suffering, gentleness, goodness, faith."

This shows that joy and peace are the fruit of the Spirit, and we cannot expect to have the fruit of the Spirit until we have received the Spirit, and we cannot receive the Spirit until we have accepted Christ. This is brought out very clearly in Eph. 1:13:

> "In whom ye also trusted, after that ye heard the word of truth, the gospel of your salvation: in whom also, *after that ye believed,* ye were sealed with that Holy Spirit of promise."

Emphasize the point that it is *after* we believe that we are sealed with the Holy Spirit of promise.

Use also Acts 5:32:

> "And we are his witnesses of these things; and so is also the Holy Ghost, whom God hath given *to them that obey him.*"

This will show that the Holy Spirit is given to those who obey Christ, and we cannot expect to receive the Holy Spirit until we have obeyed God by putting our trust in Jesus Christ and confessing Him openly before the world. A verse which will be useful in this connection as showing that it is after we confess Christ that He confesses us before the Father, is Matt. 10:32:

> "Whosoever therefore shall confess me before men, him will I confess also before my Father which is in heaven."

And so we have no right to expect the sealing of the Holy Spirit until we have confessed Christ before men.

It is after we have believed that we rejoice with joy unspeakable and full of glory, I Pet. 1:8:

"Whom having not seen, ye love; in whom, though now ye see him not, yet believing, ye rejoice with joy unspeakable and full of glory."

Our duty is believing with the heart and confessing with the mouth, leaving the matter of feeling to God; Rom. 10:10:

"For with the heart man believeth unto righteousness; and with the mouth confession is made unto salvation."

2. *"Sorrow for sin."* The feeling that many are waiting for, is a feeling of sorrow for sin. If you find this to be the case with any individual with whom you are dealing, proceed as follows:

(1) Use the passages already given to produce conviction of sin. (See Chapter VI, Section I.)

(2) Show that it is not sorrow for sin, but turning away from sin and accepting Christ that God demands. For this purpose use the following passages:

"Let the wicked forsake his way, and the unrighteous man his thoughts: and let him return unto the Lord, and he will have mercy upon him; and to our God, for he will abundantly pardon." Is. 55:7.

"But as many as received him, to them gave he power to become the sons of God, even to them that believe on his name." John 1:12.

"And they said, Believe on the Lord Jesus Christ, and thou shalt be saved, and thy house." Acts 16:31.

"Then Peter said unto them, Repent, and be baptized every one of you in the name of Jesus Christ for the remission of sins, and ye shall receive the gift of the Holy Ghost." Acts 2:38.

XIV. "I have been seeking Christ but cannot find Him."

1. It is well oftentimes to say to one who raises this difficulty "I can tell you just when you will find Christ." This will probably awaken surprise, but insist, "Yes, I can tell you just when you will find Christ. If you will turn to Jeremiah 29:13, you will find the exact time when you will find Christ." Then let him read:

"And ye shall seek me, and find me, *when ye shall search for me with all your heart.*"

"Now this verse tells the time when you will find Christ, when is it?" "When ye shall search for me with all your heart." "The fact is, up to this time, you have not been seeking for Him with all your heart. Are you ready to let go of everything else and seek Him to-day with all your heart?" This passage has been used in a great many cases to lead out one who has been seeking Christ for years, into a real acceptance of Him.

2. It is well sometimes to say to one who raises this difficulty, "Then you are seeking Christ? Well, did you know that Christ also is seeking you?" Then turn to Luke 19:10 (or Luke 15:3–10) and read. "Now you say you are seeking Christ, and Christ says He is seeking you, how long ought it to take for you to find one another? Will you just come to Christ and trust Him here and now?"

3. Sometimes the best thing to do is to say, "Well, if you are earnestly seeking Christ, let me show you how to find Him." Then deal with the inquirer in the way described in Chapter V.

XV. "Christians are so inconsistent."

This is one of the most common difficulties that we meet. Probably the best passage to use is Rom. 14:12:

"So then every one of us shall give account of himself to God."

When a person raises this difficulty, you can say, "So you are troubled about the sins of Christians; let me show you from God's own Word what He says about that." Then have him read the passage. When he has read the passage, ask, "Who does God say you will have to give an account of?" "Myself." "Not of inconsistent Christians then?" "No." "Are you ready to give an account of yourself to God?" The mere reading of this verse without comment, has led many who have been dwelling upon the inconsistency of others, to see themselves lost and undone before God, and to turn and accept Christ right there.

Another useful passage is Rom. 2:1–5. Hand it to the inquirer and ask him to read it carefully. When he has read it, ask him if this passage does not describe him, if he is not judging others for doing the very things he does himself. Then ask him what God says about those who judge others for what they are doing themselves. Ask him further what God says in the third verse that such a person will not escape. Ask him what the fourth verse tells him that he is really doing; and then ask him what the fifth verse tells him he is treasuring up for himself.

In many cases Matt. 7:1–5 will be found useful.

XVI. "There is some one I cannot forgive."

This is often the difficulty even when it is not stated. I have frequently found that when people told me they could not accept Christ and did not know why, the real difficulty was here, there was some one who had wronged them, or who they thought had wronged them, and they would not forgive him.

1. The first thing to do with such a one is to say, *"You must forgive or perish."* To prove this, use Matt. 6:15:

"But if ye forgive not men their trespasses, neither will your Father forgive your trespasses."

Follow this up with Matt. 18:21–35:

2. Say to the person, *"The wrong they have done you is nothing to the wrong you have done Jesus Christ."* Here use Eph. 4:32:

"And be ye kind one to another, tender-hearted, forgiving one another, even as God for Christ's sake hath forgiven you."

You might also use Matt. 18:23–35:

3. Next show the inquirer that he can forgive the other in Christ's strength. Use for this purpose Phil. 4:13, and Gal. 5:22, 23:

"I can do all things through Christ which strengtheneth me."
"But the fruit of the Spirit is love, joy, peace, long-suffering, gentleness, goodness, faith, meekness, temperance: against such there is no law."

XVII. "A professed Christian has done me a great wrong."

1. First you can reply by saying, *"That is no reason why you should wrong Christ; has He wronged you?"* Use Jer. 2:5:

"Thus saith the Lord, What iniquity have your fathers found *in me,* that they are gone far from me, and have walked after vanity, and are become vain?"

Ask the inquirer if he has found any evil in Christ, that that is what God is asking Him. One night I turned to an aged man and asked him if he was a Christian. He replied no, that he was a backslider. I asked him why he had backslidden, and he said Christian people had treated him badly. I opened my Bible and read Jer. 2:5 to him, and asked him, "Did you find any iniquity in God; did

God not treat you well?" With a good deal of feeling the man admitted that God had not treated him badly. I held him right to this point of God's treatment of him and not man's, and his treatment of God. It is well to follow this passage up with Is. 53:5 as bringing out very vividly just what Christ's treatment of us has been.

2. In the next place you can say to the one who raises this difficulty, *"The fact that a professed Christian has done you a great injury is no reason why you should do yourself a greater injury by refusing Christ and losing eternal life and being lost forever."* Then you can say, "Let me show you what injury you are doing yourself by rejecting Christ." Use for this purpose Jno. 3:36, and II Thess. 1:7–9:

> "He that believeth on the Son hath everlasting life; and he that believeth not the Son shall not see life; but the wrath of God abideth on him."
>
> "And to you who are troubled rest with us, when the Lord Jesus shall be revealed from heaven with his mighty angels, in flaming fire taking vengeance on them that know not God, and that obey not the gospel of our Lord Jesus Christ."

XVIII. "I have done a great wrong and will have to make it right and cannot."

1. *Tell the inquirer to take Christ first, and leave the matter of settling the wrong with Him,* that he cannot settle the matter as it ought to be settled until he has first taken Christ. Make it very plain that the only thing God requires of a sinner is to accept Christ, and all other questions must be left until that point has been settled. Use John 3:36 for this purpose, and Acts 10:43.

2. Show him further that *if there is any wrong to be made right, Christ will give him strength to make it right,* and use for this purpose Phil. 4:13.

XIX. "I have sinned away the day of grace."

This is a very serious difficulty. It often arises from a poor state of health and a morbid condition of mind, but I have never found a case that would not yield to prayerful and judicious treatment. The best passage to use, and one that generally proves sufficient, is Jno. 6:37, the last clause:

"Him that cometh to me I will in no wise cast out."

It is oftentimes necessary to read it over and over and over again, sometimes for days and days. Hold the inquirer to the one thought that God says He is ready to receive any one who will come, urging him to come now.

Another useful passage is Rom. 10:13:

"For *whosoever* shall call upon the name of the Lord shall be saved."

Dwell upon the "whosoever."

The case of Manasseh as recorded in II Chron. 33:1–13 is useful as showing the extent to which one can go and yet how God will receive them to Himself, if they only humble themselves before him.

Luke 23:39–43 is oftentimes useful as showing how one was saved even in the hour of death.

XX. "It is too late."

This difficulty is very much like the preceding one, and the same passage, Jno. 6:37, is also useful in this case. Oftentimes, however, Deut. 4:30, 31 will prove more helpful:

"When thou art in tribulation, and all these things are come upon thee, *even in the latter days,* if thou turn to the Lord thy God, and shalt be obedient unto his voice; (for the Lord thy God is a merciful God;) he will not forsake thee, neither destroy thee, nor forget the covenant of thy fathers which he sware unto them."

In using the passage, emphasize the thought, "even in the latter days."

Still another passage is II Pet. 3:9:

"The Lord is not slack concerning his promise as some men count slackness; but is long suffering to us-ward, *not willing that any should perish,* but that all should come to repentance."

It shows that God is not willing that any should perish, and that the reason why He delays His judgment is that men may be brought to repentance.

Luke 23:39–43 is useful as showing that one was saved even as late as his dying hour, and Rev. 22:17 tells us that *whosoever will* may take of the water of life freely.

XXI. "I have committed the unpardonable sin."

1. The first thing to do in this case is to *show just what the unpardonable sin is.* For this purpose use Matt. 12:31, 32, noting the context. This passage taken in its context makes it plain that the unpardonable sin is blasphemy against the Holy Ghost, and that blasphemy against the Holy Ghost consists in deliberately attributing to the devil, the work which is known to have been wrought by the Holy Spirit. Having shown just what the unpardonable sin is, ask the inquirer, "Have you done this? Have you deliberately attributed the work which you knew to be done by the Holy Spirit to the devil?" In almost every case, if not in every case, it will be found that the inquirer has not done this.

2. Having shown what the unpardonable sin is, and that the inquirer has not committed it, *use John 6:37* as in the preceding case. Even if the inquirer thinks that he has committed the blasphemy against the Holy Ghost, use John 6:37. Ask the inquirer what Jesus Christ says about those who come to Him, and then ask him if he will come to Christ right now. If he says, "I have committed the unpardonable sin," reply that it does not say, "Him that has not committed the unpardonable sin that comes to me I will in no wise cast out," but, "Him that cometh to me, I will in no wise cast out," and put the question again, "Will you come?" To every new excuse that arises, simply repeat the promise, "Him that cometh to me I will in no wise cast out," and repeat the question, "Will you come?" If he raises some new difficulty as probably he will, simply say, "Jesus says, 'Him that cometh to me, I will in no wise cast out,' will you come?" Repeat and repeat and repeat, over and over again, until this promise is fairly burned into the heart praying all the time for the Holy Spirit to carry it home. A man was once sent to me who was in the depths of despair. He had attempted suicide some five times. He felt that he had sinned away the day of grace, and committed the unpardonable sin, and that the devil had entered into him as he did into Judas Iscariot. Day after day I dealt with him, always using Jno. 6:37. To every excuse and difficulty he would bring up I would simply say, "Jesus says, 'Him that cometh to me I will in no wise cast out." I met him at last one day for a final conflict. I said to him, "Do you believe what Jesus says?" He replied, "Yes, I believe everything in the

Bible." "Well," I said, "did not Jesus say, 'Him that cometh to me I will in no wise cast out'?" "Yes," he replied. I said, "Will you come?" He replied, "I have committed the unpardonable sin." I said, "Jesus did not say, 'If any man has not committed the unpardonable sin, and comes to me I will in no wise cast him out'; He said, 'Him that cometh to me I will in no wise cast out'; will you come?" He said, "I am possessed of the devil." I replied, "Jesus did not say, 'If a man is not possessed of the devil and comes to me I will in no wise cast him out'; He said, 'Him that cometh to me, I will in no wise cast out'; will you come?" He said, "The devil has actually entered into me." I replied, "Jesus did not say, 'If the devil has not entered into a man and he comes to me I will in no wise cast him out'; He said, 'Him that cometh to me, I will in no wise cast out'; will you come?" He said, "My heart is too hard to come." I replied, "Jesus did not say, 'If a man's heart is not too hard and he comes to me, I will in no wise cast him out'; He said, 'Him that cometh to me, I will in no wise cast out'; Will you come?" He said, "I don't feel like coming." I replied, "Jesus did not say, 'If any man feels like coming, and comes to me, I will in no wise cast him out'; He said, 'Him that cometh to me, I will in no wise cast out'; will you come?" He said, "I don't know that I can come in the right way." I replied, "Jesus did not say, 'If any man cometh unto me in the right way, I will in no wise cast him out'; He said, 'Him that cometh to me, I will in no wise cast out'; will you come?" He said, "I do not know that I want to come." I replied, "Jesus did not say, 'He that wants to come, and comes to me I will in no wise cast out'; He said, "Him that cometh to me, I will in no wise cast out'; will you come?" He said, "I don't know that I know how to come." I replied, "Jesus did not say, 'He that knows how to come, and comes to me I will in no wise cast out'; He said, 'Him that cometh to me I will in no wise cast out'; will you come? Will you get down here now and come just the best you know how?" Hesitatingly the man knelt down. I asked him to follow me in prayer. I prayed about as follows: "Lord Jesus, thou hast said 'Him that cometh to me, I will in no wise cast out'; now the best I know how, I just come." The man repeated the words after me. I said, "Did you really come?" "Yes," he said, "I did." Then I said, "What has Jesus done? Never mind what you feel, but what does Jesus say He has done? 'Him that cometh to me I will in no wise cast out.' What has Jesus done, what does He say He has done?" He replied, "He has received me." I said, "Are you willing to stand there on the naked Word of God?" He replied, "I am." "Now," I said, "you are going to your room. I have no doubt that the devil will give you an awful fight, but will you stand right there on the word of Jesus, 'Him that cometh to me, I will in no wise cast out'?" He replied, "I will." He went to his room. The devil did come and assail him, and try to get him to look at his own heart, his own feelings, and his doubts, but he kept looking to the promise of Jesus, "Him that cometh to me, I will in no wise cast out"; he believed that naked promise, he came out of his struggle a victor. This was eight or nine years ago. To-day he is one of the most useful men in America.

XXII. Heb. 6:4-6.

"For it is impossible for those who were once enlightened, and have tasted of the heavenly gift, and were made partakers of the Holy Ghost, and have tasted the good word of God, and the powers of the world to come, *if they shall fall away to renew them again unto repentance;* seeing they crucify to themselves the Son of God afresh, and put him to an open shame."

Very many men and women are in deep distress of soul over this passage. They fear that it describes them, and that there is no hope of their salvation. The way to deal with such a person is to explain to him the exact meaning of the passage.

1. Show him first of all, that it is addressed to Hebrew Christians who were in danger of *apostatizing, renouncing Christ* and going back to Judaism. Then ask him if this describes his case. Of course he will say that it does not. Furthermore show him that it does not describe a person who has merely fallen in sin, but one who has *fallen away,* that is apostatized, and deliberately renounced Christ. Ask him if this describes his case. In most cases, of course, it will be found that it does not.

2. In the next place show him that the difficulty is not that God is not willing to receive such a one back, but that it is impossible "to renew them again unto repentance." That is, that their hearts are utterly hardened, and they have no desire to come to Christ. Then show him that this does not describe his case, the

very fact of his being in anxiety and burden of heart proving that it does not.

3. Sometimes all of this fails, if so, simply go over the fourth verse, and ask him if that has really been his experience, if he has actually been made a partaker of the Holy Ghost.

4. Show him by the case of Peter that one who has been a follower of Christ may fall into deep sin, and yet be restored and become more useful than ever. Use for this purpose, Luke 22:31, 34, Mark 14:66–72, Jno. 21:15–19.

5. Finally use Jno. 6:37, as described above.

XXIII. Heb. 10:26, 27.

"For *if we sin wilfully after that we have received the knowledge of the truth, there remaineth no more sacrifice for sins,* but a certain fearful looking for of judgment and fiery indignation, which shall devour the adversaries."

Many are troubled by this passage just as others are troubled by Heb. 6:4–6. I have met many in deepest anguish because they thought that this described their experience. The way to deal with such a one is to show him exactly the meaning of the verse. Explain to him that the word "wilfully" means deliberately, and of stubborn choice. It is the same word that is translated "willingly" in I Pet. 5:2. It does not describe a man who in weakness falls into sin, but a man who, with his whole heart, rejects obedience to God and the service of Christ, and throws himself with all his soul into sin. Ask him if this describes his case. Finally use Jno. 6:37.

XXIV. "God seems to me unjust and cruel."

1. The shortest way of dealing with many who say this, is to take them at once to Rom. 9:20:

"Nay but, O man, *who art thou that repliest against God?* Shall the thing formed say to him that formed it, Why hast thou made me thus?"

Apply the verse directly to the inquirer's case. Ask him if he realizes who God is, and who he himself is, and say, "You are replying against God. You are accusing God of sin. Now this is God's message to you, 'Nay but, O man, who art thou that repliest against God?' " This verse has been used of the Holy Spirit to break down in repentance and tears many a man who has complained against God.

This may be followed up by Rom. 11:33:

> "O the depth of the riches both of the wisdom and knowledge of God! *how unsearchable* are his judgments, and his ways past finding out!"

Show the inquirer that the reason God seems to him to be unjust and cruel is because such is the depth of the riches both of the wisdom and knowledge of God, and so unsearchable are His judgments, that he cannot find them out.

This can be followed up still further by Is. 55:8, 9:

> "For my thoughts are not your thoughts, neither are your ways my ways, saith the Lord. For as the heavens are higher than the earth, so are my ways higher than your ways, and my thoughts than your thoughts."

Another excellent passage to use is Job 40:2:

> "Shall he that *contendeth with the Almighty* instruct him? *he that reproveth God,* let him answer it."

When the complainer has read the verse, ask him if he wishes to contend with the Almighty. Show him further that he is reproving God, and God says he must answer for it; ask him if he is ready to answer for it.

2. *If the inquirer is complaining of God's cruelty because of some sorrow or anguish in his own life,* it is well to use Heb. 12:5–7, 10–12:

> "And ye have forgotten the exhortation which speaketh unto you as unto children, My son, despise not thou the chastening of the Lord, nor faint when thou art rebuked of him; for whom the Lord loveth he chasteneth, and scourgeth every son whom he receiveth.
>
> "If ye endure chastening, God dealeth with you as with sons; for what son is he whom the father chasteneth not?"
>
> "For they verily for a few days chastened us after their own pleasure; but he for our profit, that we might be partakers of his holiness.
>
> "Now no chastening for the present seemeth to be joyous, but grievous; nevertheless afterward it yieldeth the peaceable fruit of righteousness unto them which are exercised thereby.
>
> "Wherefore lift up the hands which hang down, and the feeble knees."

One should deal very tenderly with a case like this, yet at the same time faithfully. Show the inquirer that the sorrows and disappointments and afflictions that he has suffered are God's loving dealings with him, to bring him into a life of holiness and higher joy, that God does not willingly afflict.

One can follow the above passage with Is. 63:9:

"In all their affliction he was afflicted, and the angel of his presence saved them; in his love and in his pity he redeemed them; and he bare them, and carried them all the days of old."

In order to lead the sorrow-stricken soul to see that the sufferings of this present time are not worthy to be compared with the glory which shall be revealed in us, use Rom. 8:18:

"For I reckon that the sufferings of this present time are not worthy to be compared with the glory which shall be revealed in us."

Another useful passage is II Cor. 4:17, 18:

"For our light affliction, which is *but for a moment,* worketh for us a far more exceeding and eternal weight of glory; while we look not at the things which are seen, but at the things which are not seen: for the things which are seen are temporal; but the things which are not seen are eternal."

3. Sometimes it is well to say in such a case, "You would not think that God was unjust and cruel if you only realized the depth of your own sin against Him," and use Matt. 22:37, 38 to show him the greatness of his sin, in the way described in Chapter VI.

4. It is a wise plan to follow up all the preceding methods by showing the complainer the wonderful love of God. Jno. 3:16 and Is. 53:5 will serve well for this purpose.

XXV. "I cannot see why it was necessary that Christ should die in order that men be saved."

There are very many who will tell you this. Of course those who say this are frequently mere triflers, and trying to find a hiding place from God's truth and their own duty, but some say this with a good deal of sincerity of purpose. I have found one of the most effective passages to use in such a case to be Rom. 9:20. It is well to follow this up by showing the doubter the greatness and depth of his own sin in the way described in Chapter VI. No man after he has been led by the Word of God and His Spirit to see himself as God sees him, will any longer have any difficulty with God's way of salvation, but will be only too glad to find that a sin-bearer has been provided for him.

XXVI. "There are so many things in the Bible that I cannot under-stand."

1. The first step in such a case is to show the objector why he cannot understand. A good passage to use for this purpose is I Cor. 2:14:

"But the natural man receiveth not the things of the Spirit of God: for they are foolishness unto him: neither can he know them, because they are spiritually discerned."

It can be used in this way: when the man has said, "There are so many things in the Bible that I cannot understand," reply, "Yes, that is just what the Bible says." Then show the man the passage, and say to him, "This verse tells you just why you cannot under-stand what is in the Bible, because 'the natural man receiveth not the things of the Spirit of God: for they are foolishness *unto him,*' and I suppose that many of them appear like foolishness to you." "Yes." "This verse tells you why it is, 'because they are spiritually discerned.' The truth is, you are spiritually blind. If you will turn from sin and accept Christ, you will get spiritual sight, and then many things which you cannot understand now will become as plain as day."

Is. 55:8, 9 can also be used:

"For my thoughts are not your thoughts, neither are your ways my ways, saith the Lord. For as the heavens are higher than the earth, so are my ways higher than your ways, and my thoughts than your thoughts."

You can say to the one with whom you are dealing, "This tells why you cannot understand God's truth. Why is it?" "Because His thoughts are higher than my thoughts."

Dan. 12:10 is also useful:

"Many shall be purified, and made white, and tried; but the wicked shall do wickedly: and *none of the wicked shall understand;* but the wise shall understand."

Before the man reads it, you can say to him, "I can show you a passage in the Bible that tells you just exactly why you cannot understand, and also how you can understand." When he has read it, ask him who it is that does not understand. "The wicked." "And who shall understand?" "The wise."

A passage which can also be used to good effect is II Pet. 3: 16–18:

> "As also in all his epistles, speaking in them of these things; in which are some things hard to be understood, which they that are unlearned and unstable wrest, as they do also the other scriptures, unto their own destruction. Ye therefore, beloved, seeing ye know these things before, beware lest ye also, being led away with the terror of the wicked, fall from your own steadfastness."

I Cor. 13:11, 12 and Rom. 11:33 can also be used.

2. The second step is to show how to understand. Jno. 7:17 makes this as plain as day:

> "*If any man will do his will,* he shall know of the doctrine, whether it be of God, or whether I speak of myself."

Follow this up with Ps. 119:18, and James 1:5:

> "Open thou mine eyes, that I may behold wondrous things out of thy law."
> "If any of you lack wisdom, let him ask of God, that giveth to all men liberally, and upbraideth not; and it shall be given him."

XXVII. "I cannot believe."

We will take up skeptics more at length in Chapter XI. At this point we take up the matter merely as an honest difficulty that some find in the way of accepting Christ.

1. When one states this as a difficulty, it is often well to ask him what he cannot believe. A man once said to Mr. Moody, "I cannot believe." Mr. Moody said, "Whom can't you believe?" He replied, "I cannot believe." "Whom can't you believe, can't you believe God?" "Yes," the man replied, "I can believe God, but I cannot believe myself." Mr. Moody said, "I don't want you to believe yourself, I want you to believe God." Oftentimes the difficulty is with some doctrine that has nothing directly to do with salvation; for example, a man will say, "I cannot believe the account of creation given in the first chapter of Genesis, and I can-

not believe the story about Jonah and the whale." Now of course a
man ought to believe the Bible account of creation given in the
first chapter of Genesis, and he ought to believe the story about
Jonah, but these are not questions to discuss with an unsaved
man. When a man states some such difficulty as this, the best thing
to do is to say, "Can you believe in Jesus Christ?" "Yes, I can believe in Jesus Christ." "But will you believe in Him, will you accept Him as your Saviour, your sin-bearer, and your Lord and
Master?" Show the man that it does not say, believe this doctrine
or that doctrine and thou shalt be saved, or this incident or that
incident in the Bible, but "believe on the Lord Jesus Christ and
thou shalt be saved." For this purpose use Acts 16:31, and Jno. 3:
16:

> "And they said, *Believe on the Lord Jesus Christ,* and thou shalt be
> saved, and thy house."
> "For God so loved the world, that he gave his only begotten Son, that
> whosoever *believeth in him* should not perish, but have everlasting life."

After the man has really believed on Christ and been saved, and
grown somewhat in Christian knowledge, he will be in a position
to take up secondary questions. Many a well-meaning worker
makes a great mistake in discussing secondary questions with an
unsaved man, when he is in no position to understand them at all,
but should be held to the vital point of the acceptance of Jesus
Christ as a Saviour and Lord and Master.

2. In many cases, perhaps in most cases, when one says, "I
cannot believe," the real difficulty that lies back of their inability
to believe, is unwillingness to forsake sin, and it is well to say to
such a person, "Is your unbelief the real difficulty, is there not
some sin in your life that you are unwilling to give up?" I was once
called to deal with a man, and was told that he was a skeptic, and
needed help along that line. I said to him, "Are you a skeptic?" He
replied, "Yes." I asked him what made him a skeptic, and he said
because he could not see where Cain got his wife. I said to him,
"Is that your real difficulty?" "Yes." I replied, "Then if I remove
that difficulty, and show you where Cain got his wife, will you
become a Christian?" He said, "Oh, no, I cannot promise that."
"But," I said, "you said that was your difficulty, the thing that
kept you from accepting Christ; now if I remove that difficulty,

and you are honest, of course you will accept Christ." The man laughed and saw that he was cornered. "Now," I said, "let me ask you a question; is not the real difficulty some sin in your life?" The man broke down and confessed that it was, and he told me what the sin was, and professed to give it up and accept Christ then and there. When you are convinced that the real difficulty in the case is sin, a good passage to use is Jno. 5:44:

> "How can ye believe, which receive honor one of another, and seek not the honor that cometh from God only."

Say to the man before he reads it, "Yes, I suppose you cannot believe, but Jesus Christ tells us just why it is that men cannot believe," and then have him read the passage. Then you can say to him, "The reason why you cannot believe according to this verse, is because you are seeking the honor that comes from man and not the honor that comes from God alone. Is this not so?" Be courteous, but do not let the inquirer dodge that point.

Is. 55:7 is also a good passage to use:

> "Let the wicked forsake his way, and the unrighteous man his thoughts: and let him return unto the Lord, and he will have mercy upon him; and to our God, for he will abundantly pardon."

This will show the man that he not only needs to forsake his way, but his thoughts as well, and that if he will, and return to the Lord, He will have mercy upon him and abundantly pardon.

3. Finally in dealing with this difficulty, it is well to show a man how to believe. You can say to him after you have dealt with him along the lines already mentioned, "I can show you how to believe." Then give him Jno. 7:17:

> "If any man *will do his will,* he shall know of the doctrine, whether it be of God, or whether I speak of myself."

Ask him if he will be willing to do the will of God, if he will surrender his will to God. Then show him James 1:5–7:

> "If any of you lack wisdom, *let him ask of God,* that giveth to all men liberally, and upbraideth not; and it shall be given him. But let him ask in faith, nothing wavering. For he that wavereth is like a wave of the sea driven with the wind and tossed. For let not that man think that he shall receive any thing of the Lord."

Follow this up with John 20:31:

"But *these are written*, that ye might believe that Jesus is the Christ, the Son of God; and that believing ye might have life through his name."

Then give him the Gospel of John to study prayerfully. We will go into this more at length in Chapter XI.

CHAPTER VIII

HOW TO DEAL WITH THOSE WHO ENTERTAIN FALSE HOPES

I. The hope of being saved by a righteous life.

1. This is the most common of false hopes. Even among those who profess to be Christians, there are many who are really depending upon their lives as Christians for their acceptance before God. Those who are depending upon their righteous lives for salvation, are readily known by their saying such things as this: "I am doing the best I can." "I do more good than evil." "I am not a great sinner." "I have never done anything very bad." This mistake can be directly met by Gal. 2:16:

> "Knowing that a man is not justified by the works of the law, but by the faith of Jesus Christ, even we have believed in Jesus Christ, that we might be justified by the faith of Christ, and not by the works of the law: for *by the works of the law shall no flesh be justified.*"

After the passage has been read, you can say to the one with whom you are dealing, "Now you are expecting to be justified and accepted before God by what you are doing, by your own life and character; but God tells you in this passage, that 'by the works of the law shall no flesh be justified.'" Follow this up by Rom. 3:19, 20:

> "Now we know that what things soever the law saith, it saith to them who are under the law: that every mouth may be stopped, and all the world may become guilty before God. Therefore *by the deeds of the law there shall no flesh be justified in his sight:* for by the law is the knowledge of sin."

Call attention to the fact that here again we are told that, "by the deeds of the law there shall no flesh be justified in his sight," and

THOSE WHO ENTERTAIN FALSE HOPES   91

furthermore, that the purpose of the law is to stop the mouths of men. Then take him to Gal. 3:10:

> "For *as many as are of the works of the law are under the curse:* for it is written, Cursed is every one that continueth not in all things which are written in the book of the law to do them."

Before he reads it, say to him, "I want you to read a verse from the Word of God that tells you just how God regards one who is trying to be saved by his righteous life, as you are." Then let him read the passage. When he has read the passage, ask him where God says that he is, and hold him to the point until he sees that in depending upon his good deeds for salvation, he is under the curse.

James 2:10 will also be found useful:

> "For whosoever shall keep the whole law, and yet *offend in one point,* he is guilty of all."

Before the man reads the verse you can say, "Well, if you are going to be saved by your righteous life, let us see what God requires in order that a man may be saved on that ground." After he has read the verse, show him that if he is going to be saved by the law, he must keep the whole law, for if he offends in one point he is guilty of all.

A verse which is useful in showing the kind of righteousness that God demands, is Matt. 5:20:

> "For I say unto you, That except your righteousness shall exceed the righteousness of the scribes and Pharisees, ye shall in no case enter into the kingdom of heaven."

This verse shows that no man's righteousness comes up to God's standard, and if a man wishes to be saved, he must find some other way of salvation than by his own deeds. It is sometimes well in using this passage, to say to the inquirer, "You do not understand the kind of righteousness God demands, or you would not talk as you do. Now let us turn to God's own Word and see what kind of righteousness it is that God demands."

2. There is another way of dealing with this class, by using such passages as these:

> "And he said unto them, Ye are they which justify yourselves before men; but God *knoweth your hearts:* for that which is highly esteemed among men is abomination in the sight of God." Luke 16:15.

"In the day when *God shall judge the secrets of men* by Jesus Christ according to my gospel." Rom. 2:16.

"But the Lord said unto Samuel, Look not on his countenance, or on the height of his stature; because I have refused him: for the Lord seeth not as man seeth; for man looketh on the outward appearance, but *the Lord looketh on the heart.*" I Sam. 16:7.

These passages show that God looks at the heart. Hold the inquirer right to that point. Every man, when brought face to face with that, must tremble, for he knows that whatever his outward life may be, his heart will not stand the scrutiny of God's all-seeing and holy eye. No matter how self-righteous a man may appear, we need not be discouraged, for somewhere in the depths of every man's heart is the consciousness of sin, and all we have to do is to work away until we touch that point. Every man's conscience is on our side.

3. Matt. 22:37, 38 can also be used with those who expect to be saved by their righteous lives. You can say to the man, "If you expect to be saved by your righteous life, you are greatly deceived, and certainly entertain a false hope. For so far from living a righteous life, you have broken the very first and greatest of God's commandments." Of course he may not believe this at first, but you can turn him to the passage mentioned, and show him what the first and greatest of God's commandments is, and ask him if he has kept it. This passage is especially useful if a man says, "I am doing the best I can," or if he says, "I am doing more good than evil." You can say to him, "You are greatly mistaken about that. So far from doing more good than evil, you have broken the first and greatest of God's laws," and then show him the passage.

4. A fourth method of dealing with this class is to use Heb. 11:6 and Jno. 6:29:

"But *without faith* it is impossible to please him: for he that cometh to God must believe that he is, and that he is a rewarder of them that diligently seek him."

"Jesus answered and said unto them, *This* is the work of God, *that ye believe on him whom he hath sent.*"

These passages show that the one thing which God demands is faith, that the work of God is to believe on Him whom He hath sent, and that without faith it is impossible to please God whatever else a man may possess. John 16:9 can also be used to show that unbelief in Christ is the greatest sin:

"Of sin, *because they believe not on me.*"

5. Still another way of dealing with this class is by the use of Jno. 3:36:

"He that believeth on the Son hath everlasting life: and he that believeth not the Son shall not see life; but the wrath of God abideth on him."

This shows that the gift of eternal life depends solely upon a man's acceptance of Jesus Christ. That the sin which brings the heaviest punishment is that of treading under foot the Son of God, can be shown by Heb. 10:28, 29:

"He that despised Moses' law died without mercy under two or three witnesses: of how much sorer punishment, suppose ye, shall he be thought worthy, who hath trodden under foot the Son of God, and hath counted the blood of the covenant, wherewith he was sanctified, an unholy thing, and hath done despite unto the Spirit of grace?"

Before using this passage, it is well to say, "You think you are very good, but do you know that you are committing the most awful sin in God's sight which a man can commit?" If he replies, "I do not think so," then tell him, "Let me show you from God's Word that you are." Then turn to this passage and read it with great solemnity and earnestness.

A very useful passage with many a self-righteous man is Luke 18:10–14. You can say to the man, "There is a picture in the Bible of a man just like you, who expected to be accepted before God on the ground of his righteousness, and who had, as men go, much righteousness to present to God, but let us see what God says to him." Then have him read the passage.

It is well to bring all those who expect to be saved by a righteous life into the presence of God, for in His holy presence self-righteousness fades away. (See Is. 6:5 and Job 42:5, 6.) But how shall we bring any one into the presence of God? By opening to them passages that reveal the holiness of God, and by praying the Holy Spirit to carry these passages home. It is also well whenever possible, to get the inquirer to pray. Many a man who is stoutly maintaining his excellence before God, has given way when he has been brought to get down on his knees in God's very presence.

II. "God is too good to damn any one."

This is what another class of those who entertain false hopes think.

1. When any one says this, you can reply, "We know nothing about God's goodness, except what we learn from the Bible. If we give up the Bible, we have no conclusive proof that God is love, and can therefore build no hopes upon His goodness. But if we accept the Bible statement that God is love, we must also accept the Bible representations of the goodness of God. Let us then go to the Bible and find out the character of God's goodness." Then turn the inquirer to Rom. 2:4, 5:

> "Or despisest thou the riches of his goodness and forbearance and long suffering; *not knowing that the goodness of God leadeth thee to repentance?* But after thy hardness and impenitent heart treasurest up unto thyself wrath against the day of wrath and revelation of the righteous judgment of God."

When the man has read the verse, you can say to him, "This verse tells us what the purpose of God's goodness is; what is it?" "To lead us to repentance." "And what does this verse tell us will be the result if we do not permit the goodness of God to lead us to repentance, but trample it under foot and make it an excuse for sin?" He will find the answer to this question in verse five, and hold him to it until he sees it, that if we despise the riches of His goodness, then we are treasuring up unto ourselves "wrath against the day of wrath and revelation of the righteous judgment of God." You can also use Jno. 8:21, 24 and Jno. 3:36 to show the man that however good we may be, if we do not believe in Jesus with a living faith, we shall die in our sins, and not go where Jesus is, and that we shall not see life, but that the wrath of God abideth upon us.

2. Still another way to deal with this man is to show him that it is not so much God who damns men, as men who damn themselves in spite of God's goodness, because they will not repent and come to Christ and accept the life freely offered. For this purpose use II Pet. 3:9–11:

> "The Lord is not slack concerning his promise, as some men count slackness; but is long suffering to us-ward, *not willing that any should perish,* but that all should come to repentance. But the day of the Lord

will come as a thief in the night; in the which the heavens shall pass away with a great noise, and the elements shall melt with fervent heat, the earth also and the works that are therein shall be burned up. Seeing then that all these things shall be dissolved, what manner of persons ought ye to be in all holy conversation and godliness?"

Another good passage to use in this way is Jno. 5:40:

"*And ye will not come* to me, that ye might have life."

Press the thought of this text home, that if any one does not obtain life, it is because he will not come to Christ, and that men therefore are damned in spite of God's goodness if they will not come to Christ and accept life. In much the same way one can use Eze. 33:11:

"Say unto them, As I live, saith the Lord God, I have no pleasure in the death of the wicked; but that the wicked turn from his way and live: turn ye, turn ye from your evil ways; for why will ye die, O house of Israel?"

It is sometimes well to say, "You are right in thinking that God is not willing to damn any one; furthermore He offers life freely to you, but there is one difficulty in the way. Let us turn to Jno. 5:40 and see what the difficulty is." When he has read it, you can say, "You see now, that the difficulty is not that God wishes to damn you, but that you will not come to Christ that you might have life."

3. If these methods do not succeed, II Pet. 2:4-6, 9 may prove effectual:

"For if *God spared not the angels that sinned,* but cast them down to hell, and delivered them into chains of darkness, to be reserved unto judgment; and spared not the old world, but saved Noah the eighth person, a preacher of righteousness, bringing in the flood upon the world of the ungodly; and turning the cities of Sodom and Gomorrha into ashes condemned them with an overthrow, making them an ensample unto those that after should live ungodly;
"The Lord knoweth how to deliver the godly out of temptations, and to reserve the unjust unto the day of judgment to be punished."

Before using the passage you can say, "The best way to judge what God will do is not by speculating about it, but by looking at what He has done in the past." Then turn to these passages and let him read. When he has read it, ask him, "What did God do with the angels that sinned?" "What did He do with the world of the ungodly in the days of Noah?" "What did He do with the wicked in the days of Sodom and Gomorrha? What then may you expect Him to do with you in spite of any theories that you may have about His character and actions." This should all be done not in a controversial way, but with great earnestness, tenderness and solemnity. You can say still further, "God has not left us to speculate as to what He will do with the persistently impenitent, He has told us plainly in Matt. 25:41, 46":

> "Then shall he say also unto them on the left hand, Depart from me, ye cursed, into everlasting fire, prepared for the devil and his angels:
> "And these shall go away into everlasting punishment: but the righteous into life eternal."

You may say still further that God does bear long with man, but His dealings with man in the past show that at last His day of waiting will end, and in spite of man's doubt of His word, and doubt of his severity in dealing with the persistently impenitent, He does at last punish. You might use II Chron. 36:11–21 as an illustrative case in point.

4. It is well sometimes to add to all the other passages, Jno. 3:18, 19:

> "He that believeth on him is not condemned: but he that believeth not is condemned *already*, because he hath not believed in the name of the only begotten Son of God. And this is the condemnation, that light is come into the world, and men loved darkness rather than light, because their deeds were evil."

Before having the inquirer read the verses, you can say, "You say God is too good to damn any one, but the truth is that you are condemned already. It is not a question of what is going to happen to you in the future, but a question of your present position before God." When he has read the passage, ask him, "When is it that the one who believeth not is condemned?" "Already." "Why is it that he is condemned?" "Because light is come into the world, and he loves darkness rather than light."

5. Luke 13:3 is very effective in some case, for it shows how the "good" God deals with persons who persist in sin. The passage can be used in this way: "You say God is too good to damn any one, but let us see what God Himself says in His Word." Then turn to the passage and read, "Except ye repent, ye shall all likewise perish." Repeat the passage over and over again until it has

been driven home. An earnest missionary in the western part of New York was once holding meetings in a country village. The Universalist minister of the place was very anxious to engage the missionary in a controversy, but the missionary always said that he was too busy for controversy. One day the Universalist minister came into the house where the missionary was calling; he was delighted to see him, for he thought that his opportunity for a discussion had come at last. He began the customary universalist argument about God being too good to damn any one. After he had gone through the usual volume of words, the missionary simply replied, "I am too busy for argument, but I just want to say to you, that except you repent, you shall likewise perish." The Universalist was somewhat angry, but replied sneeringly, "That is not argument, it is simply a quotation from the Bible," and then ran on with another stream of words. When he had finished his second speech, the missionary simply replied, "I have no time for argument, but I just want to say to you, except you repent, you shall likewise perish." Again the Universalist sneered and poured forth another torrent of what he called argument. When he had finished this time the missionary again said, "I have no time for controversy, I simply want to say to you that except you repent, you shall likewise perish. Now I must go, but let me say, you will not be able to forget what I have said." The Universalist preacher laughed, and said he guessed he would forget it quick enough, that the missionary had used no argument whatever, but had simply quoted the Bible. The following day there was a knock at the missionary's door, and when it was opened, the Universalist preacher came in. The missionary said, "I have no time for argument." "Oh, sir!" said the other, "I have not come to argue with you. You were right yesterday when you told me there was one thing I would not be able to forget; I feel that it is true, that except I repent I must perish, and I have come to ask you what I must do to be saved." The missionary showed the man the way of life, and the result was, the Universalist became a real believer in Christ, and a preacher of the truth he had previously labored to pull down.

III. "I am trying to be a Christian."

The third class of those who entertain false hopes, are those who say, "I am trying to be a Christian."

1. Show the inquirer that it is trusting and not trying that saves. For this purpose use Is. 12:2:

> "Behold, God is my salvation; *I will trust,* and not be afraid: for the Lord Jehovah is my strength and my song; he also is become my salvation."

When he has read it, ask him what it is the prophet says, "I will try?" "No, I will trust." Another verse which can also be used to show that it is not trying to be a Christian, but believing on Christ that saves, is Acts 16:31:

> "And they said, Believe on the Lord Jesus Christ, and thou shalt be saved, and thy house."

Jno. 1:12 is very useful. Before using it, you can say, "What God asks of you is not to try to be a Christian, or to try to live a better life, or to try to do anything but simply to receive Jesus Christ who did it all." Then have the passage read and say to the inquirer, "Will you now stop your trying, and simply receive Jesus as a Saviour?" Make it very clear what this means and hold the inquirer to this point.

2. Another way of dealing with this class is to show the inquirer that it is *not trying* what we can do, *but trusting* what Jesus has done that saves from guilt. Use for this purpose Rom. 3:23–26:

> "For all have sinned, and come short of the glory of God; being justified freely by his grace through the redemption that is in Christ Jesus: whom God hath set forth to be a propitiation through faith in his blood, to declare his righteousness for the remission of sins that are past, through the forbearance of God; to declare, I say, at this time his righteousness: that he might be just and *the justifier of him which believeth in Jesus.*"

When the inquirer has read the passage, ask him if this teaches us that we are justified by trying to do something. "No." "Then how are we justified?" Hold him to it until he says, "Freely by His grace, through the redemption that is in Christ Jesus," and sees that it is on the simple condition of faith. Another very effective passage to use in the same way is Rom. 4:3–5:

> "For what saith the scripture? Abraham believed God, and it was counted unto him for righteousness. Now to him that worketh is the reward not reckoned of grace, but of debt. But *to him that worketh not, but believeth* on him that justifieth the ungodly, *his faith* is counted for righteousness."

This makes it clear as day that it is not our trying, but our believing on Him that justifies us. Acts 10:43 and 13:38 can be used in a similar way.

3. It is also well to show the inquirer that it is not our trying in our own strength, but our trusting in Christ's strength that saves from the power of sin. To make this clear, use the following passages:

> "Now unto him that is able to keep you from falling, and to present you faultless before the presence of his glory with exceeding joy." Jude 24.
>
> "For whatsoever is born of God overcometh the world: and this is the victory that overcometh the world, even our faith. Who is he that overcometh the world, but he that believeth that Jesus is the Son of God?" I John 5:4, 5.
>
> "For the which cause I also suffer these things: nevertheless I am not ashamed: for I know whom I have believed, and am persuaded that he is able to keep that which I have committed unto him against that day." II Tim. 1:12.
>
> "Who are kept by the power of God through faith unto salvation ready to be revealed in the last time." I Pet. 1:5.

IV. "I feel saved", or "I feel that I am going to heaven."

There are very many in this class, very many who think that their entrance into heaven is sure because they "feel saved," or feel that they are going to heaven.

1. The first thing to do with this class is to show them the utter unreliability of our feeling as a ground of hope. An excellent passage for this purpose is Jer. 17:9:

> "The heart is deceitful above all things, and desperately wicked: who can know it?"

Follow this up with Prov. 14:12:

> "There is a way *which seemeth right* unto a man, but the end thereof are the ways of death."

After reading the latter passage, you can say to the inquirer, "The way you are going seems to be right, it seems to you as if it would lead to heaven, but what does this passage tell us about a way that seemeth to be right unto a man?" "The end thereof are the ways of death." Then drive the thought home that it will not do to rest our hope upon anything less sure than the Word of God. Luke 18:9–14 may be used in this way. You can say, "We are told in the

Bible about a man who felt saved, and felt sure of going to heaven, let us read about him." Then let him read the story of the Pharisee, and show how he was not saved for all his self-confidence. Is. 55:8 can also be used to enforce the thought that God's thoughts are not our thoughts, and while we may think we are saved, God may clearly see that we are not.

2. Having shown how little confidence is to be put in our feeling, show the true ground of hope, namely God's Word. Use for this purpose Titus 1:2:

> "In hope of eternal life, which God, that cannot lie, promised before the world began."

You can say, "Paul had a hope of eternal life. Upon what was that hope built?" "The Word of God 'that cannot lie.'" Then say to the person, "Do you want a hope built upon that sure ground?" Take him then to John 3:36. That verse tells clearly how to get such a hope. One afternoon I was speaking to a woman who a few weeks before had lost her only child. At the time of the child's death she had been especially interested, but her serious impressions had largely left her. After a time I put to her the question, "Do you not wish to go where your little one has gone?" She replied, "I expect to." "What makes you think that you will," I asked. She answered, "I feel so: I feel that I will go to heaven when I die." I then asked her if there was anything she could point to in the Word of God which gave her a reason for believing that she was going to heaven when she died. She replied that there was not. She then turned to me and began to question me: "Do you expect to go to heaven when you die?" "Yes, I know I shall." "How do you know it? Have you any word from God for it?" "Yes," I answered, and turned to Jno. 3:36. She was then led to see the difference between a faith that depended upon her feeling, and a faith that depended upon the Word of God.

V. **The hope of being saved by a mere profession of religion, or by a faith that does not save from sin and lead to repentance.**

In many communities it is very common to meet men and women who believe they are saved because they hold to an orthodox creed, or because they have been baptized or made a profession of religion. This is one of the most dangerous of all false hopes, but it can be readily dealt with.

1. A good passage to begin with is Titus 1:16:

> "They profess that they know God; but in works they deny him, being abominable, and disobedient, and unto every good work reprobate."

You can say to the person, "You profess to know God, but God Himself tells us that many who profess to know Him are lost; let me show it to you in His Word." When they have read the verse, you can say, "Now if one professes to know God, but denies Him in his life, what does God Himself say that such a one is?" "Abominable and disobedient, and unto every good work reprobate." Another passage which can be used in very much the same way is Matt. 7:21, 22, 23.

> "Not every one that saith unto me Lord, Lord, shall enter into the kingdom of heaven; but he that doeth the will of my Father which is in heaven. Many will say to me in that day, Lord, Lord, have we not prophesied in thy name? and in thy name have cast out devils? and in thy name done many wonderful works? And then will I profess unto them, I never knew you: depart from me, ye that work iniquity."

You might say, "God tells us plainly in His Word that one may make a profession of religion, may be active even in Christian work, and yet be lost after all." Then have him read the verses. When they are read, you can say, "According to these verses, will a mere profession of religion save any one?" "No, doing the will of the Father which is in heaven." "Are you doing His will?"

2. A second way of dealing with this class is to say, "God tells us plainly that in order to be saved we must be born again." Then show them John 3:3–5:

> "Jesus answered and said unto him, Verily, verily, I say unto thee, Except a man be born again, he cannot see the kingdom of God. Nicodemus saith unto him, How can a man be born when he is old? can he enter the second time into his mother's womb, and be born? Jesus answered, Verily, verily, I say unto thee, Except a man be born of water and of the Spirit, he cannot enter into the kingdom of God."

When these verses are read, you can say, "Now these verses make it clear, that in order to enter the kingdom of God, one must be born again. Now let us turn to other parts of the Bible and see what it is to be born again." For this purpose use the following:

"Whosoever is born of God *doth not commit sin,* for his seed remaineth in him: and he cannot sin, because he is born of God." I John 3:9.

"If ye know that he is righteous, ye know that *every one that doeth righteousness* is born of him." I John 2:29.

"Therefore if any man be in Christ, *he is a new creature:* old things are passed away; behold, all things are become new." II Cor. 5:17.

3. A third method of dealing with this class is by saying, "Yes, faith does indeed save, but it is a certain kind of faith that saves." To show what the faith that saves is, turn to Gal. 5:6:

"For in Jesus Christ neither circumcision availeth any thing, nor uncircumcision; but *faith which worketh by love.*"

This passage says that it is faith which worketh by love. Rom. 10: 9, 10 that it is a faith of the heart:

"That if thou shalt confess with thy mouth the Lord Jesus, and shalt believe *in thine heart* that God hath raised him from the dead, thou shalt be saved. For *with the heart* man believeth unto righteousness; and with the mouth confession is made unto salvation."

while James 2:14 tells us that it is faith which shows itself in works:

"What doth it profit, my brethren, though a man say he hath faith but have not works? can that faith save him?" (R. V.)

4. I Jno. 5:4, 5 is also very useful as showing that one who really has faith in Jesus as the Son of God, and is born of God, overcomes the world. The passage reads as follows:

"For whatsoever is born of God *overcometh the world;* and this is the victory that overcometh the world, even our faith. Who is he that overcometh the world, but he that believeth that Jesus is the Son of God?"

The fact that one is living in sin and not overcoming the world, but being overcome by it, is conclusive proof that he really has not faith that Jesus is the Son of God, and that he has not been born of God.

CHAPTER IX

HOW TO DEAL WITH THOSE
WHO LACK ASSURANCE

It is not enough that a man be saved: to be of the most use to God he must know that he is saved, and no small part of our work as personal workers will be to lead into assurance of salvation, men and women who do not as yet know that they are saved. There are two classes of those who lack assurance.

I. Those who lack assurance because of ignorance.

1. There are many who lack assurance for the simple reason that they do not know that it is any one's privilege to know that they have eternal life. Oftentimes if you ask people if they know that they are saved, or if they know that their sins are forgiven, they reply, "Why no, no one knows that." You can say, "Yes, the Bible says that all who believe may know it," and then show them I Jno. 5:13:

> "These things have I written unto you that believe on the name of the Son of God; *that ye may know* that ye have eternal life, and that ye may believe on the name of the Son of God."

It is well to begin with this passage, and not to leave it until it becomes very clear that it is every believer's privilege to know that he has everlasting life. Follow this up with Jno. 1:12:

> "But as many as received him, to them gave he power to become the sons of God, even to them that believe on his name."

This verse shows that Christ gives to as many as receive Him, power to become the sons of God. A good way to use this verse is to ask the inquirer questions regarding it. "What does every one who receives Him receive power to become?" "A son of God."

"Are you sure that every one who receives Jesus obtains power to become a son of God?" "Yes." "What makes you sure." "God says so here." "Have you received Jesus?" "Yes." "What then have you received power to become?" Just hold the inquirer to the point that it is not what he feels he has power to become, but what God here in His Word says he has power to become. It will usually be necessary to go through it again and again and again.

Jno. 3:36 can be used in a similar way. "He that believeth on the Son hath everlasting life." Ask the inquirer, "Who does this verse say has everlasting life?" "He that believeth on the Son." "How many that believe on the Son have everlasting life?" "Why, every one." "Are you sure of that?" "Yes." "Why?" "Because God says so here." "What is it God says?" "He that believeth on the Son hath everlasting life." "Does God merely say that he that believeth on the Son 'shall have' everlasting life?" "No, He says he 'hath' it. "Do you believe on the Son?" "I do." "What then does God say you have?" In a little while he will see it and say, "Everlasting life." Then have him say it over and over again, "I have everlasting life, I have everlasting life." Have him stand by it because God says so, and then have him kneel down and thank God for giving him everlasting life. Do not let the inquirer go while he continues to say, "I hope I have everlasting life." Insist upon his resting absolutely upon what God says. One night I found a young man upon his knees in great distress at the close of an evening service. I showed him from the Bible how Jesus Christ had borne his sins, and asked him if he would accept Christ as his Saviour. He said he would, and seemed to do it; but he seemed to get no light, and went out of the meeting in deep distress still. The next night he was there again, professing to accept Christ, but with no assurance that his sins were forgiven. I tried to show him from John 3:36 what God said of those who believed on the Son, but the light did not come. Finally he rose to leave the room. As he turned to leave me he said, "Will you pray for me?" I said, "Yes." He walked a few steps down the aisle and I called after him, "Do you believe I will pray for you?" He turned toward me with a look of astonishment, and said, "Yes, of course." I said, "Why do you think I will pray for you?" "Because you said so." I said, "Is not God's Word as good as mine?" He saw it at once, that while he was willing to believe my word, he was not willing to believe

God's Word. He received assurance on the spot and knew that he had everlasting life.

Another verse which can be used to advantage with this class is Jno. 5:24:

"Verily, verily, I say unto you, He that heareth my word, and believeth on him that sent me, hath everlasting life, and shall not come into condemnation; but is passed from death unto life."

This verse has been used of God to bring many into assurance of salvation. I Jno. 5:12 is also very plain:

"He that hath the Son hath life; and he that hath not the Son of God hath not life."

Acts 13:39 has been greatly used of God in dealing with this class. "By him all that believe are justified from all things, etc." Ask the inquirer, "What does this verse say that all who believe are?" "Justified." "Justified from what?" "From all things." "Do you believe?" "I do." "What are you then?" It will probably be necessary to go over it several times before the inquirer answers, "I am justified"; but when he does, tell him to thank God for justifying him, and to confess Christ before the world. See to it that he does it. I was dealing one night with a young woman who was in great distress of soul because she could not see that she had forgiveness of sin. I went carefully over the ground to find if she really had accepted Christ, and it appeared clear that she had. Then I had her read Acts 13:39, "By him all that believe are justified from all things." "Now," I said, "Who does God say in this verse are justified from all things?" "All that believe." "Believe on whom?" "Believe on Christ." "Do you believe on Christ?" "I do." "Have you really accepted Him as your Saviour and Lord and Master?" "Yes." "Then you are sure you believe on Him?" "Yes." "And what does this verse say that all who believe are?" "Justified." "What then are you?" She would not say, "I am justified," but wept over the thought that her sins were not forgiven. I went over it again and again and again. At last the simple meaning of the words seemed to dawn upon her darkened mind. I asked her as before, "Who does God say are justified?" "All that believe." "From what are they justified?" "From all things." "Who is justified from all things?" "All that believe." "Who says so?" "God says so." "Do you believe?" "I do." "What are you then?" A joyous light spread over her countenance, and she said, "Why I am justified from all things," and immediately she turned toward her friend standing near and said to me, "Now won't you speak to my friend about Christ?"

2. Many inquirers of this class stumble over the fact that they have not the witness of the Holy Spirit. Show them that the witness of the Word to their acceptance is sufficient from I Jno. 5:10:

"He that believeth on the Son of God hath the witness in himself: he that believeth not God hath made him a liar; *because he believeth not the record that God gave* of his Son."

This verse tells us that if we believe not the witness of God, in His Word, we make Him a liar. I was once dealing with a very intelligent young man along this line. He professed that he had accepted Jesus Christ, but that he did not know that he had eternal life. I showed him God's testimony that "he that hath the Son hath life." (I Jno. 5:12.) "Now," I said, "You have the Son." "Yes." "And God says that he that hath the Son hath what?" "Life." Then I read the tenth verse, "He that believeth not God hath made Him a liar; because he believeth not the record that God gave of His Son." "Now," I said, "God's record concerning His Son is that eternal life is in Him," (verse II), and that "he that hath the Son hath life," (verse 12). Now this is God's record. If you do not believe it, no matter what your feelings are, what are you doing?" In a little while the man replied, "I am making God a liar, but I never saw it before." Then and there he trusted the naked Word of God, and went out with the knowledge that his sins were forgiven, and that God had given him eternal life.

Also show those who are waiting for the witness of the Holy Spirit, that it is after we believe the testimony of the Word that we are sealed with the Holy Spirit of promise, using Eph. 1:13 for this purpose:

"In whom ye also trusted, after that ye heard the word of truth, the gospel of your salvation: in whom also *after that ye believed*, ye were sealed with that holy Spirit of promise."

The natural order in assurance is this: First, assurance of our justification, resting upon the naked Word of God (such passages as Acts 13:39); second, public confession of Christ with the mouth (Rom. 10:10); and third, the witness of the Holy Spirit (Eph. 1:13, Rom. 8:16). The trouble with many is that they wish to invert this order, and have the witness of the Holy Spirit before they confess Christ with the mouth.

It is very important in using these texts to make clear what saving faith is, because many say that they believe, when they do not in the sense of these texts, and so get a false assurance, and entertain false hopes, and never get deliverance. There is a good deal of careless dealing with those who lack assurance. Workers are so anxious to have inquirers come out clearly that they urge them on to assurance when they have no right to assurance because they have not really accepted Christ. It is better for a man not to have assurance that he is saved, than for a man to have assurance that he is saved when in reality he is not. Jno. 1:12, II Tim. 1:12 and Rom. 10:10 make very clear what the character of saving faith is.

II. Those who lack assurance because of sin.

Oftentimes the trouble with those who lack assurance is, that there is some sin or questionable practice in their lives which they ought to confess and give up. When this is the case, it will not do to deal with the inquirer along the lines mentioned above. Take him rather to such passages as John 8:12:

> "Then spake Jesus again unto them, saying, I am the light of the world: he that followeth me shall not walk in darkness, but shall have the light of life."

When the man has read the passage you can tell him that Jesus' promise was that if we follow Him we shall have the light of life. Say to him, "You have not the light of life, so the probability is that you are not following Him. Are you following Him?" Push the inquirer along this line to find if there is not some point in which he is untrue to Christ, or to the leading of the Holy Spirit. One night in an after-meeting, I was passing around here and there asking different ones about their Christian experience. A gentleman and his wife, friends from another church, had come down to the meeting. I noticed the gentleman looked at his wife as much as to say, "Speak to her." In a little while I came around to her, and asked her how she was getting on in her Christian life. She replied that she was all in the dark. I simply quoted Jno. 8:12 and passed on, but the arrow went home. She and her husband stayed after every one else had gone, and I had a private conversation with her. I asked her if she was rebelling against the will of God at any place. She confessed that she was, that her husband had received a great anointing of the Holy Spirit and she had not, and what was more, she was afraid her husband would go into Christian work and she did not want him to, and so she had gotten utterly in the dark. After some conversation and prayer, she surrendered wholly to the will of God, and the next morning received a wonderful baptism with the Holy Spirit.

Is. 55:7 is a good passage to use with those who lack assurance because of sin. Prov. 28:13 and Ps. 32:1–5 are good passages to use with those who have some unconfessed sin that is keeping them out of the enjoyment of fellowship with God. These passages show that when sin is forsaken and confessed we receive pardon and light and assurance.

Oftentimes it is well when one lacks assurance, first, to put the question clearly to him, "Do you know of any sin which you are cherishing, or anything in your life which your conscience troubles you about?"

CHAPTER X

HOW TO DEAL WITH BACKSLIDERS

One of the largest classes found in the inquiry room, and in all personal work in our day, are those who are, or call themselves backsliders. They are not all alike by any means, and they ought not all to have the same treatment. There are two classes of backsliders:

I. Careless backsliders, those who have no great desire to come back to the Saviour.

1. There is perhaps no better passage to use with such than Jer. 2:5:

> "Thus saith the Lord, What iniquity have your fathers found in me, that they are gone far from me, and have walked after vanity, and are become vain?"

Drive God's question contained in the text right home to their hearts, "What iniquity have you found in the Lord?" Dwell upon God's wonderful love to them, and show them the base ingratitude and folly of forsaking such a Saviour and friend. Very likely they have wandered away because of the unkind treatment of some professed Christian, or of some minister, but hold them right to the point of how the Lord treated them, and how they are now treating Him. Use also Jer. 2:13:

> "For my people have committed two evils; they have forsaken me the fountain of living waters, and hewed them out cisterns, broken cisterns, that can hold no water."

Have the inquirer read the verse, and ask, "Is not that verse true? What does the Lord say that you forsook when you forsook Him?" "The fountain of living waters." "And to what does He say you turned?" "Broken cisterns that can hold no water." "Is not that true in your experience? Did you not forsake the fountain of living waters, and have you not found the world broken cisterns that can hold no water?" I have yet to find the first backslider of whom this is not true and I have used it with many. Then illustrate the text by showing how foolish it would be to turn from a fountain of living water to broken cisterns or muddy pools. If this verse does not accomplish the desired result, use Jer. 2:19:

> "Thine own wickedness shall correct thee, and thy backslidings shall reprove thee: know therefore and see that it is an evil thing and bitter, that thou hast forsaken the Lord thy God, and that my fear is not in thee, saith the Lord God of hosts."

When they have read it, ask them if they have not found in it an "evil thing and bitter" that they have forsaken the Lord their God. It is well sometimes to go over the misfortunes and troubles that have come since they forsook the Lord, for it is a fact as every experienced worker knows, that when a man who had had a real knowledge of Christ backslides, misfortune after misfortune is likely to overtake him. Prov. 14:14, the first half of the verse, is also a good passage to use:

> "The backslider in heart shall be filled with his own ways."

I Kings 11:9 can also be used:

> "And the Lord was angry with Solomon, because his heart was turned from the Lord God of Israel, which had appeared unto him twice."

One of the best passages to show the folly and evil results of backsliding is Luke 15:13–17. Go into detail in bringing out the point of the picture here given of the miseries that came to the backslider in the far country.

2. It is well sometimes to use Amos 4:11, 12:

> "I have overthrown some of you, as God overthrew Sodom and Gomorrha, and ye were as a firebrand plucked out of the burning: yet have ye not returned unto me, saith the Lord. Therefore thus will I do unto thee, O Israel: and because I will do this unto thee, prepare to meet thy God, O Israel."

Before the passage is read you can say, "There is a passage in the Old Testament that contains a message from God to backsliding Israel, and I believe it is a message for you also. Then have him read the passage carefully and after he has read it, ask him what the message of God to backsliding Israel was. "Prepare to meet thy God." Then say to him, "It is God's message to you too, as a backslider tonight, to 'prepare to meet thy God.'" Go over this again and again until the thought rings in the heart of the man.

II. Backsliders who are sick of their wandering and sin, and desire to come back to the Lord.

These are a very different class from those just mentioned, though of course they are related. They are perhaps as easy a class to deal with as we ever find. There are many who once had a knowledge of the Lord who have wandered into sin, and who are now sick and tired of sin, and are longing to come back, but think that there is no acceptance for them. Point them to Jer. 3:12, 13, 22:

> "Go and proclaim these words toward the north, and say, Return, thou backsliding Israel, saith the Lord; and I will not cause mine anger to fall upon you: for I am merciful, saith the Lord, and I will not keep anger forever. Only acknowledge thine iniquity, that thou hast transgressed against the Lord thy God, and hast scattered thy ways to the strangers under every green tree, and ye have not obeyed my voice, saith the Lord. "Return, ye backsliding children, and I will heal your backslidings. Behold we come unto thee; for thou art the Lord our God."

This will show them how ready the Lord is to receive them back, and that all He asks of them is that they acknowledge their sin and return to Him.

Hos. 14:1-4, is full of tender invitation to penitent backsliders, and also shows the way back to God.

> "O Israel, return unto the Lord thy God; for thou hast fallen by thine iniquity. Take with your words, and turn to the Lord: say unto him, Take away all iniquity, and receive us graciously: so will we render the calves of our lips. Asshur shall not save us; we will not ride upon horses: neither will we say any more to the work of our hands, Ye are our gods: for in thee the fatherless findeth mercy. I will heal their backsliding, I will love them freely: for mine anger is turned away from him."

I use this passage more frequently than almost any other with the class of whom we are speaking, especially the first and fourth verses. I show them first of all that God is inviting the backslider to Himself, and second that He promises to heal their backsliding and love them freely, and third, that all that He asks is that they take words of confession and return to Him (verse 2). The following verses all set forth God's unfailing love for the backslider, and His willingness to receive him back:

"But thou hast not called upon me, O Jacob; but thou hast been weary of me, O Israel.

"Thou hast bought me no sweet cane with money, neither hast thou filled me with the fat of thy sacrifices: but thou hast made me to serve with thy sins, thou hast wearied me with thine iniquities. I, even I, am he that blotteth out thy transgressions for mine own sake, and will not remember thy sins." Is. 43:22, 24, 25.

"He feedeth on ashes: a deceived heart hath turned him aside, that he cannot deliver his soul, nor say, Is there not a lie in my right hand? Remember these, O Jacob and Israel; for thou art my servant: I have formed thee; thou art my servant: O Israel, thou shalt not be forgotten of me. I have blotted out, as a thick cloud, thy transgressions, and, as a cloud, thy sins: *return unto me; for I have redeemed thee.*" Is. 44: 20-22.

"For I know the thoughts that I think toward you, saith the Lord, thoughts of peace, and not of evil, to give you an expected end. Then shall ye call upon me, and ye shall go and pray unto me, and I will hearken unto you. And ye shall seek me, and find me, when ye shall search for me with all your heart." Jer. 29: 11–13.

"And there ye shall serve gods, the work of men's hands, wood and stone, which neither see, nor hear, nor eat, nor smell." Deut. 4:28.

"(For the Lord thy God, is a merciful God;) he will not forsake thee, neither destroy thee, nor forget the covenant of thy fathers which he sware unto thee." Deut. 4:31.

"If my people, which are called by my name shall humble themselves, and pray, and seek my face, and turn from their wicked ways, then will I hear from heaven, and will forgive their sin, and will heal their land." II Chron. 7:14.

One of the most useful verses in dealing with an intelligent backslider who wishes to return to the Lord is, I Jno 1:9:

"If we confess our sins, he is faithful and just to forgive us our sins and to cleanse us from all unrighteousness."

It is well sometimes to follow this up with I Jno. 2:1, 2:

"My little children, these things write I unto you, that ye sin not. And if any man sin, we have an advocate with the Father, Jesus Christ the righteous, and he is the propitiation of our sins: and not for ours only, but also for the sins of the whole world."

Often it is helpful to give illustrations of great backsliders who returned to the Lord, and how lovingly He received them. For this purpose you can use Mark 16:7:

"But go your way, tell his disciples *and Peter* that he goeth before you into Galilee: there shall ye see him, as he said unto you."

This tells of Christ's loving message to Peter after he had so grievously sinned, and deliberately denied his Master. II Chron. 15:4

and 33:1–9, 12, 13 give illustrations of great backsliders who returned to the Lord, and how lovingly He received them.

Luke 15:11–21 is perhaps the most useful passage of all in dealing with a backslider who wishes to return, for it has both the steps which the backslider must take, and also a picture of the loving reception from God that awaits him.

When a backslider returns to Christ, he should always be given instructions as to how to live so as not to backslide again. These instructions will be found in Chapter V., Sec. II.

CHAPTER XI

HOW TO DEAL WITH PROFESSED SKEPTICS AND INFIDELS

There are various classes of skeptics, and it is not wise to use the same methods in dealing with all.

I. Skeptics who are mere triflers.

A very large share of the skeptics of our day belong to this class. Their professed skepticism is only an excuse for sin, and a salve for their own consciences. As a rule it is not wise to spend much time on an individual of this class, but rather give him something that will sting his conscience and arouse him out of his shallowness. A good passage for this purpose is I Cor. 1:18:

"For the preaching of the cross is to *them that perish foolishness,* but unto us which are saved it is the power of God."

Very likely the skeptic will say, "The Gospel and the whole Bible is all foolishness to me." You can reply by saying, "Yes, that is exactly what God says." "But," the man will say, "you don't understand me, the Gospel and the whole Bible is foolishness to me." "Yes," you can reply, "that is exactly what the Bible says." The man's curiosity will be piqued, and his mind opened by his curiosity to receive a word of truth, off his guard. Then have him read I Cor. 1:18. Then you can say, "You said that the Gospel was foolishness to you, and God Himself says that 'the preaching of the cross is to them that perish foolishness,' and it is foolishness to you because you are perishing; 'but unto us which are saved it is the power of God.'" Oftentimes it will be well to leave the man without another word of comment. Be careful not to laugh at him, and not to produce the impression that you are joking; but leave him with the thought that he is indeed perishing.

II Cor. 4:3, 4 can be used in much the same way. Before the passage is read you can say to the man, "You are a skeptic because the Gospel is hidden to you, but God Himself has told us in His Word to whom the Gospel is hidden, and why it is hidden to them." Then let him read the passage:

"But *if our gospel be hid, it is hid to them that are lost:* in whom the god of this world hath blinded the minds of them which believe not, lest the light of the glorious gospel of Christ, who is the image of God, should shine unto them."

When he has read it, you can say, "That verse explains to you the secret of your difficulty. The Gospel is hidden to you because you are lost, and the reason it is hidden is because the god of this world has blinded your mind, lest the light of the glorious Gospel of Christ, who is the image of God, should shine upon you." I have also found I Cor. 2:14 useful:

"But the natural man receiveth not the things of the Spirit of God: for they are foolishness unto him: neither can he know them, because they are spiritually discerned."

I have used it to show the man that it was no more than was to be expected that the things of the Spirit of God would be foolishness unto him, because they were spiritually discerned. I was dealing one night with a very bright student. He could hardly be called altogether a trifler, for he was a young man of a good deal of intellectual earnestness. He said to me, "This is all foolishness to me." I replied by saying, "That is exactly what the Bible says." He looked very much astonished, and protested that I did not understand him, that he had said it was all foolishness to him. "Yes," I replied, "that is what the Bible says. Let me show it to you." I opened my Bible to the passage and let him read. When he had read it, I said, "That explains why it is foolishness to you; 'the natural man cannot receive the things of the Spirit of God for they are foolishness unto him.'" "Why," he said, "I never thought of that before." The Spirit of God carried it home to his heart, and the man was lead to an honest acceptance of Christ.

II Thess. 1:7–9 can be used with good results with a trifling skeptic or agnostic. If the man says in an uppish way, "I am an agnostic," you can say, "Well, God has told us a good deal about agnostics and their destiny; let us see what He has said." Then have him read this passage:

> "And to you who are troubled rest with us, when the Lord Jesus shall be revealed from heaven with his mighty angels, in flaming fire *taking vengeance on them that know not God,* and that obey not the gospel of our Lord Jesus Christ; who shall be punished with everlasting destruction from the presence of the Lord, and from the glory of his power."

When it is read you can say, "Now an agnostic is one that knows not God; and this verse tells us exactly what is the destiny of an agnostic and all those who know not God. This is God's own declaration of their destiny." Then have him read it again if he will, and if he will not, quote it to him. He may laugh at you, and if he does, the Word of God often sinks deeply into the heart, even when it is treated with a sneer.

Mark 16:16 has been found very useful in dealing with trifling skeptics; when a man says to you that he is a skeptic or an infidel, it is well sometimes to say to him, "God has said some very plain words about infidels." Then give to him the passage:

> "He that believeth and is baptized shall be saved; but he that believeth not shall be damned."

and say, "I simply want to leave that message of God with you," and pass on. Jno. 3:36 can be used in a similar way.

Sometimes it is well to say to the trifling skeptic, "I can tell you the origin of your skepticism, but I can do better, I can tell you what God says of the origin of your skepticism." Then show him Jno. 8:47:

> "He that is of God heareth God's words: ye therefore hear them not, *because ye are not of God."*

II Thess. 2:10–12 can be used in extreme cases:

> "And with all deceivableness of unrighteousness in them that perish, *because they received not the love of the truth,* that they might be saved. And for this cause God shall send them strong delusion, that they should believe a lie: *that they all might be damned who believed not the truth, but had pleasure in unrighteousness."*

You can say to the man, "There is a very interesting passage in the Bible regarding skeptics. It tells what is the origin of their skepticism and what is the outcome of it." Then have him read the passage. When he has read it say, "Now what does this passage say about the origin of skepticism?" Show him it is "because they received not the love of the truth, that they might be saved." "What is the result of their refusal to receive the truth?" "God shall give them over to strong delusion that they shall believe a lie." "And what is the outcome of it all?" "That they all might be damned who believed not in the truth, but had pleasure in unrighteousness."

Ps. 14:1 is useful in some cases, though it needs to be used with discretion and kindness. Before giving it to the man to read, you can say, "I do not wish to say anything unkind to you, but God Himself has said a very plain word about those who say there is no God; let me show it to you." Then let him read:

"The fool hath said in his heart, There is no God."

When he has read it, say, "I am not saying that, but God has said it. Now it is a matter between you and God, but I would advise you not to forget what God has said." Of course this applies especially to one who is skeptical about, or denies the existence of God.

In dealing with a skeptic who is a trifler, and in fact with all skeptics, don't argue, don't get angry, be very gentle but very solemn, and very much in prayer, depending upon the Holy Spirit to give you words to say and to carry them home.

II. An earnest-minded skeptic.

Many skeptics are not triflers. There are very many men and women in our day who are really very desirous of knowing the truth, but who are in an utter maze of skepticism. There is no more interesting class of people to deal with than this. In beginning work with them, it is well to ask them the following preliminary questions:

1. *"What can't you believe?"* Get as full an answer as possible to this question, for many a man thinks he is a skeptic when really he does believe the great fundamental truths. Furthermore, in finding out what a man does believe, no matter how little it is, you have a starting point to lead the man out to further faith.

2. *"Why can't you believe?"* This will oftentimes show the man how utterly without foundation are his grounds for unbelief.

3. *"Do you live up to what you do believe?"* This will give you an opportunity in many cases to show a man that his trouble is not so much what he does not believe, as his failure to live up to what he does believe. Only the other night I was dealing with a man

who told me that his trouble was that he could not believe, but we had not gotten far in the conversation when it became clear to us that his trouble was not so much that he could not believe, but that he did not live up to what he did believe.

4. *"What do you believe?"* A few important lines along which to carry out this inquiry are, "Do you believe that there is an absolute difference between right and wrong?" "Do you believe that there is a God?" "Do you believe in prayer?" "Do you believe any part of the Bible, if so what part?"

Having asked the man these preliminary questions, proceed at once to show him how to believe. I have found no passage in the Bible equal to John 7:17 in dealing with an honest skeptic:

> "If any man *will do his will,* he shall know of the doctrine, whether it be of God, or whether I speak of myself."

It shows the way out of skepticism to faith, and has been used of God to the salvation of countless skeptics and infidels. You can say to the skeptic, "Now Jesus Christ makes a fair proposition. He does not ask you to believe without evidence, but He asks you to do a thing that your own conscience approves, and promises that if you do it, you will come out of skepticism into knowledge. What Jesus asks in this verse, is that you will to do God's will; that is, that you surrender your will to God. Will you do it?" When this point has been settled, next say to him, "Will you make an honest search to find out what the will of God is, that you may do it?" When this point has been settled, ask the man, "Do you believe that God answers prayer?" Very likely the skeptic will reply that he does not. You can say to him, "Well I know that He does, but of course I don't expect you to accept my opinion, but here is a possible clew to knowledge. Now the method of modern science is to follow out any possible clew to see what there is in it. You have given me a promise to make an honest search to find the will of God, and here is a possible clew, and if your promise was honest, you will follow it. Will you pray this prayer? 'O God, show me whether Jesus is thy Son or not; and if you show me that He is, I promise to accept Him as my Saviour and confess Him as such before the world.'" It is well to have him make his promise definite by putting it down in black and white. After this is done, show him still another step. Take him to John 20:31:

"But these are written, that ye might believe that Jesus is the Christ, the Son of God; and that believing ye might have life through his name."

Here we are told that the Gospel of John was written that we might believe that Jesus is the Christ, the Son of God. Tell him, "Now this Gospel is given for this purpose, to show that Jesus is the Christ the Son of God. Will you take this Gospel and read it, honestly and carefully?" Very likely he will say, "I have read it often before." You can say, "I want you to read it in a new way. Will you read it this way? Read a few verses at a time, and each time before you read, will you ask God to give you light on the passage that you are about to read, and promise that if He does, you will follow as much as you see to be true. Now when you have read the Gospel through, come back to me and tell me the result." I would again carefully go over all the points as to what he was to do. It would be well also to ask him to especially notice the following verses in the Gospel: 1:32–34; 3:2; 3:3; 3:16; 3:18, 19; 3: 32; 3:34; 3:36; 4:10; 4:14; 4:23; 4:34; 4:52, 53; 5:8, 9; 5:22–24; 5: 28, 29; 5:40; 5:44; 6:8–14; 6:19; 6:27; 6:29; 6:35; 6:40; 6:66–68; 7:17; 7:37–39; 7:45, 46; 8:12; 8:18; 8:21; 8:24; 8:31, 32; 8:34; 8:36; 8:38; 8:42; 8:47; 9:17; 9:24, 25; 9:35–39; 10:9; 10:11; 10:27–29; 10: 30; 11:25, 26; 11:43–45; 12:26; 12:32; 12:35, 36; 12:42, 43; 12:46; 12:48–50; 13:3; 13:13; 14:3; 14:6; 14:9; 14:15, 16; 14:21; 14:24; 14: 27; 15:5; 15:7; 15:9–11; 15:18, 19; 15:23–26; 16:3; 16:7–11; 16: 13, 14; 16:24; 17:3; 17:5; 17:12; 17:14; 17:22; 17:24; 17:25, 26; 18: 37; 19:6; 19:7–8; 20:8; 20:13–19; 20:24, 25; 20:27–29; 20:31; 21:24. This method of treatment if it is honestly followed by the skeptic will never fail.

If the skeptic does not believe even in the existence of God, you will have to begin one step further back. Ask him if he believes there is an absolute difference between right and wrong. If he says that he does not, which will be very rarely the case, it is just as well to tell him then and there that he is a mere trifler. If he says that he does, ask him if he will take his stand upon the right and follow it wherever it carries him. He will very likely try to put you off by saying, "What is right?" You can say to him that you do not ask him to take your conception of right, but will he take his stand upon the right and follow it wherever it carries him, and make an honest attempt to find out what the right is. Next say to him, "You do not know whether there is a God and whether He answers prayer or not. I know that there is a God and that He answers prayer; but I do not ask you to accept my opinion, but here is a possible clew to knowledge; will you follow it?" If he refuses, of course you will know at once that he is not an honest skeptic, and you can tell him so. If he is willing to try this clew have him offer this prayer, "O God, if there is any God, show me whether Jesus Christ is Thy Son or not, and if You show me that He is, I promise to accept Him as my Saviour and confess Him as such before the world," then have him proceed by reading the Gospel of John, etc., as in the former case. If the man is not an honest skeptic, this course of treatment will reveal the fact, and you can tell him that the difficulty is not with his skepticism, but with his rebellious and wicked heart. If a man says he does not know whether there is an absolute difference between right and wrong, you can set it down at once that he is bad, and turn to him and say frankly but kindly, "My friend, there is something wrong in your life. No man who is living a right life will doubt that there is an absolute difference between right and wrong. You probably know what the wrong is, and the trouble is not with your skepticism but with your sin.

A man who was a thorough-going agnostic once came to me and stated his difficulties. The man had had a very remarkable experience. He had dabbled in Unitarianism, Spiritualism, Buddhism, Theosophy, and pretty much every other ism extant. He was in a state of absolute agnosticism. He neither affirmed nor denied the existence of God. He told me that I could not help him, for his case was "very peculiar," as indeed it was, but I had Jno. 7:17 to build my hope upon, and the man seemed honest. I asked him if he believed there was an absolute difference between right and wrong, he said that he did. I asked him if he was willing to take his stand upon the right and follow it wherever it carried him. He said that he was. I called out my stenographer and dictated a pledge somewhat as follows: "I believe that there is an absolute difference between right and wrong, and I hereby take my stand upon the right to follow it wherever it carries me. I promise to make an honest search to find if Jesus Christ is the Son of God, and if I find that He is, I promise to accept Him as my Saviour and confess Him as such before the world." I handed the pledge to the man and asked him if he was willing to sign it. He read it carefully and then signed it. I then said to him, "You don't know there is not a God?" "No," he said, "I don't know that there is no God. Any man is a fool to say that he knows there is not a God. I neither affirm nor deny." "Well," I said, "I know there is a God, but that will do you no good." I said further, "You do not know that God does not answer prayer." "No," he said, "I do not know that God does not answer prayer, but I do not believe that He does." I said, "I know that He does, but that will not do you any good, but here is a possible clew to knowledge. Now you are a graduate of a British university. You know that the method of modern science is to follow out a possible clew to see what there is in it. Will you follow out this clew? Will you pray this prayer: 'O God, if there is any God, show me whether Jesus Christ is Thy Son or not, and if You show me that He is, I promise to accept Him as my Saviour and confess Him as such before the world'?" "Yes," he said, "I am willing to do that, but there is nothing in it; my case is very peculiar." I then turned to John 20:31 and read, "These are written, that ye might believe that Jesus is the Christ, the Son of God; and that believing ye might have life through his name." After reading the verse, I said, "John wrote this Gospel that 'ye might believe that Jesus is the Christ, the Son of God.' Will you take this Gospel and read it, not trying to believe it, but simply with a fair mind, willing to believe it if it approves itself to you as true?" He said, "I have read it time and time again, and could quote a good deal of it." I said, "I want you to read it in a new way; read a few verses at a time, ask God for light each time you read, and promise to act upon so much as you see to be true." This the man promised to do, but closed by saying, "There is nothing in it, my case is very peculiar." I went over again the various points and bade the man good-bye. A short time after I met him again. He hurried up to me, and almost the first words he said were, "There is something in that." I replied, "I knew that before." "Why," he said, "ever since I have done what I promised you to do, it is just as if I had been taken up to the Niagara river and was being carried along." Some weeks after I met the man again; his doubts had all gone. The teachings of the men he had formerly listened to with delight, had become utter foolishness to him. He had put himself in a way to find out the truth of God, and God had made it known to him, and he had become a believer in Jesus Christ as God's Son, and the Bible as God's Word.

There is no more interesting class, and no easier class to deal with, than honest skeptics. Many are afraid to tackle them, but there is no need of this. There is a way out of skepticism into faith laid down in the Bible that is absolutely sure if any one will take it. As for skeptics who are triflers, it is not best to spend much time on them, but simply to give them some searching passages of Scripture, and to look to the Spirit of God to carry the Word home.

III. Special classes of skeptics.

1. *Those who doubt the existence of God.* The passages given under I. and II. may be used with this class, and usually it is wise to use them before the specific passages given under this head.

(1) An excellent passage to use with those who claim to doubt the existence of God is Rom. 1:19–22:

> "Because that which may be known of God is manifest in them; for God hath shewed it unto them. For the invisible things of him from the creation of the world are clearly seen, *being understood by the things that are made,* even his eternal power and Godhead; so that they are without excuse: because that, *when they knew God, they glorified him not as God, neither were thankful;* but became vain in their imaginations, and their foolish heart was darkened. Professing themselves to be wise, they became fools."

Ask the doubter to read this passage carefully. When he has done so, you can say to him, "Of course you never saw God, but this verse tells us how the invisible things of Him whom we have never seen can be known, and how is it?" "By the things that are made." "What does Paul say we can understand by the things that are made?" "His eternal power and Godhead." "Is not this true, do not the facts of nature prove an intelligent creator?" It is well sometimes to illustrate by a watch or something of that sort. Show the inquirer a watch and ask him if he believes it had an intelligent maker, and why he thinks so; then ask him about his eye which shows more marks of intelligence in its construction than a watch, or anything man ever made. Having dwelled upon this argument and made it clear, ask him what God says those are who do not believe in God as revealed in His works. Bring out the fact that

God says they are "without excuse." Then you can say to him, "The twenty-first verse tells us why men get in the dark about God." Have him read this verse also. "According to this verse, why is it that men get in the dark about God?" "Because that, when they knew God, they glorified him not as God, neither were thankful." "Is not this true about you? Was there not a time when you knew God, believed that there was a God, but did not glorify Him as God, neither returned thanks to Him? What does God say is the result of this course?" "They became vain in their imaginations, and their foolish heart was darkened." "Now is this not precisely your case? Has not your foolish heart been darkened by not glorifying God when you knew Him? Now the twenty-second verse describes such persons. Exactly what does it say about them?" "Professing themselves to be wise, they become fools."

In something the same way you can use Ps. 19:1, 2:

> "The heavens declare the glory of God; and the firmament sheweth his handiwork. Day unto day uttereth speech, and night unto night sheweth knowledge."

"According to this passage, what declares to us the glory of God?" "The heavens." "What shows His handiwork?" "The firmament." "Do you know anything about the stars?" Let the skeptic tell what he knows about the stars. If he knows nothing, tell him something about their greatness, their magnitude, and their wonderful movements, and then ask him if it does not indicate a wonderful creator. Endeavor to make him see that he is not honest in his denial of God.

(2) Tell him that there is still one verse you wish to give him, and that you hope he will bear in mind that it is not you who says it, but God; and that it applies to his case exactly. Then have him read the first half of Ps. 14:1:

> "The fool hath said in his heart, There is no God."

When he has read it, ask him who it is, according to this verse, who says "There is no God." "The fool." "Where is it that he says there is no God?" "In his heart." "Why is it then that the fool says there is no God, because he cannot believe in God, or because he does not wish to believe in God?" You can add that the folly of saying in one's heart there is no God is seen in two points, first, because there is a God, and it is folly to say there is not one when there is; and second, because the doctrine that there is not a God always brings misery and wretchedness. Put it right to the man, and ask him if he ever knew a happy atheist. Before leaving him, you can tell him that he is losing the greatest blessing for time and for eternity by doubting the existence of God. Turn him to Rom. 6:23 and show him that this is so:

"The wages of sin is death; but the gift of God is eternal life through Jesus Christ our Lord."

When he has read the verse, say to him, "This verse tells us that we have our choice between eternal death, which is the wages that we have earned by sin, and eternal life, which is the gift of God, but of course if we do not believe in God, we cannot look to Him for this gift." You can further tell him that in his present state of mind it is impossible for him to do anything that pleases God, and show him Heb. 11:6 and have him read it if he will, and if he will not, read it to him.

2. *Those who doubt that the Bible is the Word of God.* The method of dealing with honest skeptics described above is as a rule the best method of dealing with this class, but other plans will be useful with some.

(1) Oftentimes men say, "I do not believe the Bible as a whole is the Word of God, but I accept what Jesus Christ says." If one says this, get him to take his stand clearly and definitely upon this statement, that he accepts the authority of Jesus Christ. Get him to commit himself to this point. When he has done it, say to him, "Well, if you accept the authority of Jesus Christ, you must accept the authority of the whole Old Testament, for Jesus Christ has set the seal of His authority to the entire book." This the man will not believe at first, but turn him to Mark 7:13; show him the context, thereby proving to him that Jesus here calls the law of Moses the Word of God. Then say to him, "If you accept the authority of Jesus, you must accept the authority of at least the first five books of the Bible as being the Word of God. You can follow this up by Matt. 5:18:

"For verily I say unto you, Till heaven and earth pass, one jot or one tittle shall in no wise pass from the law till all be fulfilled."

Here Jesus sets His authority to the absolute inerrancy of the Old Testament law. Then turn him to John 10:35:

> "If he called them gods unto whom the word of God came, and *the Scripture cannot be broken.*"

Show him that here Jesus quotes a passage from the Psalms, (Ps. 82:6), and says that the Scripture cannot be broken, and hereby sets the stamp of His authority to the absolute inerrancy of the entire Old Testament Scriptures. Turn him next to Luke 24:27:

> "And beginning at Moses and all the prophets, he expounded unto them in all the scriptures the things concerning himself."

Show him from this passage how Jesus quoted the entire Old Testament Scriptures, Moses and the prophets, as being of conclusive authority. Then go on to the 44th verse, and call his attention to the fact that Jesus said that "all things must be fulfilled, which were written in the law of Moses, and in the prophets, and in the Psalms." Remind him that the Jew divided his Bible, the present Old Testament Scriptures, into three parts, the Law, the Prophets and the Psalms, and that Jesus took up each one of these parts in detail, and set the stamp of His authority upon the whole. Therefore hold him to the point that if he accepts the authority of Christ, he must accept the authority of the whole Old Testament, and he has already said that he did accept the authority of Christ.

To prove that Christ set the stamp of His authority to the New Testament, take him to Jno. 14:26:

> "But the Comforter, which is the Holy Ghost, whom the Father will send in my name, he shall teach you all things, and bring all things to your remembrance, whatsoever I have said unto you."

Here Jesus plainly declares that not only would the teaching of the apostles be true, but that it would contain all the truth, and furthermore, that their recollection of what He Himself said, would not be their own recollection, but the recollection of the Holy Ghost. Follow this up with Jno. 16:12, 13:

> "I have yet many things to say unto you, but ye cannot bear them now. Howbeit when he, the Spirit of truth, is come, he will guide you into all truth: for he shall not speak of himself; but whatsoever he shall hear, that shall he speak: and he will shew you things to come."

Show him that Jesus Himself said, "I have many things to say unto you, but ye cannot bear them now. Howbeit when He, the Spirit of truth, is come, He will guide you into all truth." Therefore, tell him that Jesus said the apostles would be taught of the Holy Spirit, that the Holy Spirit would guide them *into all the truth,* and that their teaching would be more complete than His own. "Therefore, if you accept the authority of Jesus, you must accept the authority of the entire New Testament."

(2) If the objector says that Paul never claimed that his teachings were the Word of God, turn him to I Thess. 2:13:

> "For this cause also thank we God without ceasing, because when ye received *the word of God which ye heard of us,* ye received it not as the word of men, *but as it is in truth, the word of God,* which effectually worketh also in you that believe."

(3) A passage which is useful as describing the character of Bible inspiration is II Peter 1:21:

> "For the prophecy came not in old time by the will of man: but holy men of God *spake as they were moved by the Holy Ghost.*"

I Cor. 2:14 is useful as proving verbal inspiration (see especially Am. R. V.).

(4) Sometimes it is well to say to the doubter, "The Bible itself explains why it is that you do not believe the Bible is the Word of God." Then show him Jno. 8:47. Follow this up by saying, "That you do not believe the Bible is God's word does not alter the fact," and show him Rom. 3:3, 4:

> "For what if some did not believe? shall their unbelief make the faith of God without effect? God forbid: yea, let God be true, but every man a liar; as it is written, That thou mightest be justified in thy sayings, and mightest overcome when thou art judged."

You can go further yet and say that God Himself tells us that there is awful guilt attaching to the one who will not believe the record that He has given, and then show him I Jno. 5:10:

> "He that believeth on the Son of God hath the witness in himself: *he that believeth not God hath made him a liar;* because he believeth not the record that God gave of his Son."

Ask him when he has read it, "What does God say here of the one who does not believe the record that He has given of His Son?" and make him see that God says he has made God a liar.

(5) Finally you may use Luke 16:30, 31:

"And he said, Nay, father Abraham: but if one went unto them from the dead, they will repent. And he said unto him, If they hear not Moses and the prophets, neither will they be persuaded, though one rose from the dead."

Before reading it, say, "Well, God says that the case of one who will not listen to the Bible is very desperate. Just read and see what He says upon this point," and then have him read the verse.

3. *Those who doubt the divinity of Christ.* It is very common in our day to have men say that they believe in God, but they do not believe that Jesus Christ was the Son of God. The best way, as a rule, to deal with such is along the line described in I and II, especially under II; but sometimes there is a man who has real difficulties on this point, and it is well to meet him squarely.

(1) In the first place, show such a one that we find several divine titles applied to Christ, the same titles being applied to Christ in the New Testament that are applied to Jehovah in the Old: Acts 10:36 and I Cor. 2:8, compare Ps. 24:8–10:

"'The word which God sent unto the children of Israel, preaching peace by Jesus Christ: (he is *Lord of all).*" Acts 10:36.
"Which none of the princes of this world knew: for had they known it, they would not have crucified *the Lord of glory."* I Cor. 2:8.
"Who is this King of glory? The LORD strong and mighty, the LORD mighty in battle. Lift up your heads, O ye gates; even lift them up, ye everlasting doors; and the King of glory shall come in. *Who is this King of glory? The LORD of hosts, he is the King of glory.* Selah." Ps. 24: 8–10.

Heb. 1:8; Jno. 20:28, Rom. 9:5, Rev. 1:17, compare Is. 44:6:

"But unto the Son he saith, Thy throne, O God, is for ever and ever: a sceptre of righteousness is the sceptre of thy kingdom." Heb. 1:8.
"And Thomas answered and said unto him, My Lord and my God." John 20:28.
"Whose are the fathers, and of whom as concerning the flesh Christ came, who is over all, *God blessed forever."* Rom. 9:5.
"And when I saw him, I fell at his feet as dead. And he laid his right hand upon me, saying unto me, Fear not; *I am the first and the last."* Rev. 1:17.
"*Thus saith the LORD* the King of Israel, and his redeemer the LORD of hosts; *I am the first, and I am the last,* and beside me there is no God." Is. 44:6.

(2) Show him further that offices are ascribed to Christ that only God could fill. For this purpose use Heb. 1:3, 10:

"Who being the brightness of his glory, and the express image of his person, and *upholding all things by the word of his power,* when he had by himself purged our sins, sat down on the right hand of the Majesty on high."

"And, thou, Lord, in the beginning hast *laid the foundation of the earth;* and *the heavens are the work of thine hands.*"

(3) Show him that the Bible expressly declares that Jesus Christ should be worshiped as God. Use for this purpose Heb. 1:6, Phil. 2:10, Jno. 5:22, 23, compare Rev. 5:13:

"And again, when he bringeth in the first begotten into the world, he saith, And let all the angels of God worship him." Heb. 1:6.

"That *at the name of Jesus* every knee should bow, of things in heaven, and things in earth, and things under the earth." Phil. 2:10.

"For the Father judgeth no man, but hath committed all judgment unto the Son: that all men should honour the Son, *even as they honour the Father.* He that honoureth not the Son honoureth not the Father which hath sent him." John 5:22, 23.

"And every creature which is in heaven, and on the earth, and under the earth, and such as are in the sea, and all that are in them, heard, saying, Blessing, and honour, and glory, and power, be unto him that sitteth upon the throne, *and unto the Lamb* for ever and ever." Rev. 5:13.

(4) Show him that Jesus claimed the same honor as His Father, and either He was divine, or the most blasphemous impostor that ever lived. For this purpose use Jno. 5:22, 23. Drive home the truth that the one who denies Christ's divinity puts Him in the place of a blasphemous impostor. Mark 14:61, 62:

"But he held his peace, and answered nothing. Again the high priest asked him, and said unto him, Art thou the Christ, the Son of the blessed? And *Jesus said, I am:* and ye shall see the Son of man sitting on the right hand of power, and coming in the clouds of heaven." (cf. vs. 63, 64.)

(5) In the next place show him that the Bible says the one who denies the divinity of Christ, no matter who he may be, is a liar and an antichrist. For this purpose use I Jno. 3:22, 23, compared with I Jno. 5:1, 5:

"*Who is a liar but he that denieth that Jesus is the Christ?* He is antichrist, that denieth the Father and the Son. Whosoever denieth the Son, the same hath not the Father: [but] he that acknowledgeth the Son hath the Father also."

"Whosoever believeth that Jesus is the Christ is born of God: and every one that loveth him that begat loveth him also that is begotten of him."

"Who is he that overcometh the world, but he that believeth that Jesus is the Son of God?"

I Jno. 5:10–12 shows that he who does not believe that Jesus is divine makes God a liar, "because he believeth not the record that God gave of his Son."

(6) Make it clear to the inquirer that God regards it as a matter of awful folly and guilt deserving the worst punishment to reject Christ as the Son of God. For this purpose use Heb. 10:28, 29:

> "He that despised Moses' law died without mercy under two or three witnesses: of how much sorer punishment, suppose ye, shall he be thought worthy, who hath trodden under foot the Son of God, and hath counted the blood of the covenant, wherewith he was sanctified, an unholy thing, and hath done despite unto the Spirit of grace?"

Follow this up with Jno. 8:24, which shows beyond a question that one who does not believe in the divinity of Christ cannot be saved, and Jno. 20:31, which shows that we obtain life through believing that Jesus is the Christ the Son of God.

(7) I have found that making clear the fact that Christ rose from the dead, and that this was God's seal to His claim to be divine, is very helpful in dealing with many who have doubts as to His divinity. I have also found Acts 9:20 very helpful:

> "And straightway he preached Christ in the synagogues, *that he is the Son of God.*"

I call attention to who it was in this verse that declared Jesus to be the Son of God, namely Saul of Tarsus. I then bring out what it was that led Paul to say this; that is, his actually seeing Jesus in the glory, and hearing the words that He spoke to him. Then I make it clear that one of three things is true: either Saul actually saw Jesus in the glory, or else he lied about it, or else he was deceived, being in a heated state of imagination or something of that kind. Then I show how he could not have lied about it, for men do not manufacture a lie for the sake of suffering for it thirty or thirty-five years.

Second, I show that the circumstances were such as to preclude the possibility of an optical delusion, or an overheated state of the imagination, for not only did Paul see the light, but those who were with him, and those who were with him also heard the voice speaking, though they did not hear what the voice said. Furthermore, there was a second man, Ananias, who received a commission independently to go to Saul and lay hands upon him, and his eyes would be opened, and Saul's eyes were opened, which of course could not be the result of imagination. So Saul of Tarsus must actually have seen Christ in the glory, and if he did, in the way described, it settles it beyond question that Jesus is the Son of God; so the divinity of Christ is not a theological speculation, but an established fact.

4. *Those who doubt the doctrine of future punishment, or the conscious, endless suffering of the lost.* As a rule it is not wise to discuss this difficulty with one who is not an out and out Christian. No one who has not surrendered his will and his mind to Jesus Christ is in a position to discuss the details of future punishment, but if one is skeptical on this point, though a Christian (in that he has accepted Christ as a personal Saviour), it is well to show him the teaching of God's Word. A great deal is made by those who deny the conscious, endless suffering of the lost, of the words "death" and "destruction," which are said to mean annihilation, or at least non-conscious existence. Say to such a one, "Let us see how the Bible defines its own terms." Rev. 21:8 defines what death means when used in the Scriptures as the punishment of the wicked:

> "But the fearful, and unbelieving, and the abominable, and murderers, and whoremongers, and sorcerers, and idolaters, and all liars, shall have their part in the lake which burneth with fire and brimstone: *which is the second death."*

Rev. 17:8, cf. Rev. 19:20 shows what "perdition" (same Greek word as translated elsewhere "destruction") means in the Scriptures:

> "The beast that thou sawest was, and is not; and shall ascend out of the bottomless pit, and go *into perdition;* and they that dwell on the earth shall wonder, whose names were not written in the book of life from the foundation of the world, when they behold the beast that was, and is not, and yet is." Rev. 17:8.
>
> "And the beast was taken, and with him the false prophet that wrought miracles before him, with which he deceived them that had received the mark of the beast, and them that worshiped his image. These both were cast alive *into a lake of fire burning with brimstone."* Rev. 19:20.

Rev. 17:8 tells us that the beast was to go into "perdition," (destruction), Rev. 19:20 tells us just where the beast went, "into a lake of fire burning with brimstone." This then is "perdition." But Rev. 20:10 shows us the beast still there at the end of one thousand years, *and being still consciously tormented, and to be tormented day and night forever and ever.* This then is what the Bible means by "perdition" or "destruction," conscious torment forever and ever in a lake of fire. Rev. 20:15 shows that those who are subjected to the terrible retribution here described are those who are not found written in the book of life:

"And whosoever was not found written in the book of life was cast into the lake of fire."

Matt. 10:28 shows that there is a destruction for the soul apart from the destruction for the body:

"And fear not them which kill the body, but are not able to kill the soul: but rather fear him which is able to destroy both soul and body in hell."

Luke 12:5 shows that *after one is killed* (and is of course dead), there is still punishment in hell:

"But I will forewarn you whom ye shall fear: fear him, which *after he hath killed* hath power to cast into hell; yea, I say unto you, Fear him."

Mark 3:28, 29, R. V., shows that there is such a thing as an eternal sin:

"Verily I say unto you, All their sins shall be forgiven unto the sons of men, and their blasphemies wherewith soever they shall blaspheme: but whosoever shall blaspheme against the Holy Spirit hath never forgiveness, but is guilty of *an eternal sin.*"

Luke 16:23–26 shows that the condition of the wicked dead is one of conscious torment.

Mark 14:21 shows that the retribution visited upon the wicked is of so terrible a character, that it would be better for him upon whom it is visited if he had never been born:

"The Son of man indeed goeth, as it is written of him: but woe to that man by whom the Son of man is betrayed! good were it for that man if he had never been born."

II Pet. 2:4 and Jude 6 show that hell is not a place where the inhabitants cease to exist, but where they are reserved alive for the purposes of God:

"For if God spared not the angels that sinned, but cast them down to hell, and delivered them into chains of darkness, *to be reserved unto* judgment."

"And the angels which kept not their first estate, but left their own habitation, he *hath reserved in everlasting chains* under darkness unto the judgment of the great day."

Heb. 10:28, 29 shows that while the punishment for the transgression of the Mosaic law was death, sorer punishment awaits those who have trodden under foot the Son of God.

Matt. 25:41 shows that the wicked *go* to the place prepared for the devil and his angels, and share the same endless conscious torment:

"Then shall he say also unto them on the left hand, Depart from me, ye cursed, into everlasting fire, prepared for the devil and his angels."

The character of this place and the duration of its punishment is very clearly stated in Rev. 19:20 and 20:10.

CHAPTER XII

HOW TO DEAL WITH THOSE WHO WISH TO PUT OFF A DECISION UNTIL SOME OTHER TIME

Oftentimes when you have swept away every difficulty, and the way of salvation is made as clear as day, still the inquirer is not ready to decide then and there. He wishes to put off a decision until some future time. There are several classes of those who wish to put off a decision:

I. I want to wait.

One of the largest classes is composed of those who say, "I want to wait," or "Not to-night," or "I will think about it," or "I will come to-morrow night," or some other such thing.

Give to such a person Is. 55:6:

"Seek ye the Lord *while he may be found,* call ye upon him while he is near."

When the inquirer has read the passage, ask him when it is that he is to seek the Lord. When he says, "While he may be found," ask him when that is. Make it clear that the only time when he can be absolutely sure of finding the Lord is right now. Ask him if he can be sure of finding the Lord to-morrow if he does not seek Him to-day. Sometimes it is well to give illustrations from life concerning those who put off seeking the Lord, and when the next day came it was too late to find Him.

Prov. 27:1 is also a good verse to use:

"Boast not thyself of to-morrow: for thou knowest not what a day may bring forth."

When the verse has been carefully and intelligently read (if it is not read carefully and intelligently at first, ask the one with whom you are dealing to read it again), ask him what it is that God says it is unwise to boast one's self of. "To-morrow." Ask him why it is unwise to boast one's self of to-morrow. "Because thou knowest not what a day may bring forth." Ask him if he knows what a single day will bring forth. Suggest to him some of the things that it may bring forth, and then ask him if he does not think he had better take Christ then and there.

Prov. 29:1 has often been used of the Holy Spirit to bring men to an immediate decision:

> "He, that being often reproved hardeneth his neck, shall *suddenly* be destroyed, and that without remedy."

It is well after the verse has been read to ask the one with whom you are dealing, "What becomes of the one who being often reproved hardeneth his neck?" When he answers, "He shall suddenly be destroyed," ask him if he is willing to run the risk. Or you can use Matt. 25:10–12:

> "And while they went to buy, the bridegroom came; and they that were ready went in with him to the marriage: and the door was shut. Afterward came also the other virgins, saying, Lord, Lord, open to us. But he answered and said, Verily I say unto you, I know you not."

Ask him who it was that went in to the marriage, and when he answers, "They that were ready," ask him if he is ready. Then ask him what happened afterward to those who were not ready. Ask him who those who were not ready were. Then put it to him, "Are you willing to be on the outside?"

Another excellent passage to use is Luke 12:19, 20:

> "And I will say to my soul, Soul, thou hast much goods laid up *for many years;* take thine ease, eat, drink, and be merry. *But God said* unto him, Thou fool, *this night* thy soul shall be required of thee: then whose shall those things be, which thou hast provided?"

After the verses have been read, ask, "For how many years did this man think that he had his goods laid up?" "Many years." "But what did God say to him?" "How many years do you think you have before you still? But what may God say to you? When may He say it?"

A passage especially effective in dealing with those who say, "I am not ready," is Matt. 24:44:

> "Therefore be ye also ready: for in such an hour as ye think not the Son of man cometh."

Another passage which can also be used with good effect is I Kings 18:21:

> "And Elijah came unto all the people, and said, How long halt ye between two opinions? if the Lord be God, follow him: but if Baal, then follow him."

An excellent way to use this verse is by asking the person whether he would be willing to wait a year and not have an opportunity under any circumstances, no matter what came up, of accepting Christ. When he answers, "No, I might die within a year," ask him if he would be willing to wait a month, a week, a day. Ask him if he would like God, the Holy Spirit, and all Christians to leave him alone for a day, and he not have the opportunity under any circumstances of accepting Christ. Almost any thoughtful person will say "No." Then tell him if that is the case, he had better accept Christ at once. Dr. Chalmers was the first one to use this method, and it has been followed by many others with great success.

Other passages which can be used with this class are:

> "Go to now, ye that say, To-day or to-morrow we will go into such a city, and continue there a year, and buy and sell, and get gain: whereas ye know not what shall be on the morrow. For what is your life? It is even a vapour, that appeareth for a little time, and then vanisheth away." James 4:13–14.
>
> "Because there is wrath, beware lest he take thee away with his stroke: then a great ransom cannot deliver thee." Job 36:18.
>
> Luke 13:24–28.
>
> "Then said Jesus again unto them, I go my way, and ye shall seek me, and shall die in your sins: whither I go, ye cannot come." John 8:21.
>
> "Then Jesus said unto them, Yet a little while is the light with you. Walk while ye have the light, lest darkness come upon you: for he that walketh in darkness knoweth not whither he goeth." John 12:35.
>
> "Then said Jesus unto them, Yet a little while am I with you, and then I go unto him that sent me. Ye shall seek me, and shall not find me: and where I am, thither ye cannot come." John 7:33, 34.

II. I must get fixed in business first, and then I will become a Christian."

Those who say, "I must get fixed in business first, and then I will become a Christian."

With such persons use Matt. 6:33:

> "But seek ye first the kingdom of God, and his righteousness; and all these things shall be added unto you."

This verse makes it very clear that we must seek the kingdom of God first, and everything else must be made secondary.

III. I am waiting for God's time.

Those who say, "I am waiting for God's time."

Quite frequently this is said in all honesty. Many people have an idea that God has a certain time for saving people, and we must wait until this time comes. If any one says this, ask him if he will accept Christ in God's time if you will show him just when God's time is. When he says he will, turn him to II Cor. 6:2:

> "(For he saith, I have heard thee in a time accepted, and in the day of salvation have I succoured thee: behold, *now is the accepted time*, behold, now is the day of salvation.)"

This verse shows him that God's time is now. Or turn to Heb. 3:15:

> "While it is said, *To-day* if ye will hear his voice, harden not your hearts, as in the provocation."

This shows that God's time is today.

IV. I am too young to be a Christian.

Those who say, "I am too young to be a Christian," or "I want to wait until I am older."

With such a person open your Bible to Eccl. 12:1 and read:

> "Remember now thy Creator *in the days of thy youth,* while the evil days come not, nor the years draw nigh, when thou shalt say, I have no pleasure in them."

Matt. 19:14 and 18:3 are also good passages to use, as they show that youth is the best time to come to Christ, and that all must become as children, even if they are old, before they can enter into the kingdom of heaven.

It is oftentimes wise in dealing with persons who wish to put off a decision until some time in the future to use the passages given for dealing with those who have little or no concern about their salvation (Chapter VI), until such a deep impression is made of their need of Christ that they will not be willing to postpone accepting Him. As a rule in dealing with those under I, it is best to use only one passage, and drive that home by constant repetition. One night I was dealing with a man who was quite excited, but kept saying, "I cannot decide to-night." Over and over again I quoted Prov. 29:1. In reply to every answer he made, I would give this passage. I must have repeated it a great many times in the course of the conversation, until the man was made to feel, not only his need of Christ, but the danger of delay, and the necessity of a prompt decision. He tried to get away from the passage, but I held him to this one point. The passage remained with him, and it was carried home by the providence of God, for he came nearly being destroyed on the street that night; he was assaulted. He came back to the meeting the next night with his head all bandaged, and then and there accepted Christ. The pounding he received from his assailant would probably have done him little good if the text of the Scripture had not been previously pounded into his head.

CHAPTER XIII

HOW TO DEAL WITH THE DELUDED

I. Roman Catholics.

1. Very few Roman Catholics have assurance of salvation, indeed very few understand that it is our privilege to know that we have forgiveness of sins and eternal life. A good way then to deal with a Roman Catholic is to ask him if he knows that his sins are forgiven. Very likely he will say that he does not, and that no one else knows it either. Then you can show him that it is the believer's privilege to know that he has forgiveness of sins. For this purpose use Acts 13:39, "By him all that believe *are justified,* etc." and Eph. 1:7:

> "In whom *we have* redemption through his blood, *the forgiveness of sins,* according to the riches of his grace." Eph. 1:7.

In a similar way, you can show him that it is our privilege to know that we have eternal life. For this purpose use 1 Jno. 5:13. Oftentimes when he is brought to see that it is our privilege to know that we have forgiveness of sins and eternal life, he will desire to know it too, and will begin to see that we have something that he does not possess. There is one point at which we always have the advantage in dealing with a Roman Catholic, namely, there are a peace and a power in Christianity as we know it, that there is not in Christianity as he knows it, and he can be made to appreciate the difference.

2. Another good way to deal with a Roman Catholic is to show him the necessity of the new birth, and what the new birth is. When the one with whom you are dealing tells you that he is a Roman Catholic, it is well to ask him if he has been born again. Very likely he will say that he does not know what that means

(though oftentimes Roman Catholics do talk about the new birth).
Show him Jno. 3:3–5, 7, and emphasize what Jesus says, that we
must be born again. If he asks what the new birth is, show him the
following passages:

> "Therefore if any man be in Christ, he is a new creature: old things
> are passed away; behold, all things are become new." II Cor. 5:17.
> "Whereby are given unto us exceeding great and precious promises:
> that by these ye might be *partakers of the divine nature,* having escaped
> the corruption that is in the world through lust." II Pet. 1:4.
> "Then will I sprinkle clean water upon you, and ye shall be clean: from
> all your filthiness, and from all your idols, will I cleanse you. *A new heart
> also will I give you,* and a new spirit will I put within you: and I will take
> away the stony heart out of your flesh, and I will give you an heart of
> flesh. And I will put my spirit within you, and cause you to walk in my
> statutes, and ye shall keep my judgments, and do them." Ez. 36:25–27.

Many Roman Catholics understand the new birth to mean
baptism, and oftentimes if you ask a Roman Catholic if he has
been born again, he will say "Yes," and if you ask him when, he
will tell you at his baptism. It will then be necessary to show him
that baptism is not the new birth. For this purpose use I Cor. 4:15:

> "For though ye have ten thousand instructors in Christ, yet have ye
> not many fathers: for in Christ Jesus I have begotten you through the
> gospel."

Here Paul tells the believers in Corinth that in Christ Jesus he had
begotten them through the Gospel. If the new birth meant baptism, he must have baptized them, but in I Cor. 1:14 he declares
he had not baptized them.

Or you can say, "No, baptism is not the new birth, for I can
show you a person who we are told was baptized, and yet St. Peter told him he had not been born again." Then turn to Acts 8:13:

> "Then Simon himself believed also: and when he was baptized, he con-
> tinued with Philip, and wondered, beholding the miracles and signs which
> were done."

When you have made it clear that Simon had been baptized, turn
to Peter's statement in the 21st to the 23d verses, to show that he
had not been born again. It is well to go a step further and show
the inquirer what the Biblical evidences of the new birth are. For
this purpose use the following passages:

> "If ye know that he is righteous, ye know that every one that doeth
> righteousness is born of him." I John 2:29.

"Whosoever is born of God doth not commit sin, for his seed remaineth in him: and he cannot sin, because he is born of God.

"We know that we have passed from death unto life, because we love the brethren. He that loveth not his brother abideth in death.

"But whoso hath this world's good, and seeth his brother have need, and shutteth up his bowels of compassion from him, how dwelleth the love of God in him?" I John 3:9, 14, 17.

If the inquirer is sufficiently interested, he will now want to know how to be born again. This question is answered in:

"But *as many as received him,* to them gave he power to become the sons of God, even to them that believe on his name." John 1:12.

"Being born again, not of corruptible seed, but of incorruptible, *by the word of God,* which liveth and abideth forever." I Pet. 1:23.

"Of his own will begat he us *with the word of truth,* that we should be a kind of firstfruits of his creatures." Jas. 1:18.

3. A third way of dealing with a Roman Catholic is to use Acts 3:19.

"Repent ye therefore, and be converted, that your sins may be blotted out, when the times of refreshing shall come from the presence of the Lord."

This shows the necessity of repentance and conversion in order that our sins may be blotted out. What repentance is will be shown by Is. 55:7 and Jonah 3:10:

"Let the wicked forsake his way, and the unrighteous man his thoughts: and let him return unto the Lord, and he will have mercy upon him; and to our God, for he will abundantly pardon."

"And God saw their works, that they turned from their evil way; and God repented of the evil, that he had said that he would do unto them; and he did it not."

In a similar way Acts 16:31 can be used to show that the way to be saved is by simply believing on the Lord Jesus Christ; then to show what it is to believe on the Lord Jesus Christ use Jno. 1:12 and II Tim. 1:12.

4. Another good text to use in dealing with Roman Catholics, and one which comes right at the heart of their difficulties, is I Tim. 2:5:

"For there is one God, and *one mediator between God and men,* the man Christ Jesus."

The Roman Catholic, if he is a true Roman Catholic, is always seeking some mediator besides Jesus Christ, and this verse declares expressly that there is but "one mediator between God and men, the man Christ Jesus," and not the priests or saints or the Virgin Mary or anyone else. Sometimes it is well to follow this up with I Tim. 4:1–3, but it is not well as a rule to use this passage until one has made some headway.

It is also well to show the advantage of Bible study, for as a rule the Roman Catholic does not study the Bible at all, and in many cases is practically forbidden by the priest to study it. For this purpose use Jno. 5:39; I Pet. 2:1, 2; II Tim. 3:13–17; James 1:21, 22; Ps. 1:1, 2; Josh. 1:8; Mark 7:7, 8, 13; Matt. 22:29. These texts, except the one in I Pet. 2:1, 2 are all practically the same in the Douay or Roman Catholic Bible as they are in the several Protestant translations.

5. Still another way to deal with these people is to use the same method that you would with any sinner who does not realize his need of a Saviour, and has no real concern about his salvation (see Chapters VI and XII), that is to awaken a sense that he is a sinner and needs Christ. This as a rule is the best way if you can get the Roman Catholic to listen to you.

However, many people think there is no use talking with Roman Catholics, that they cannot be brought to Christ. This is a great mistake. Many of them are longing for something they do not find in the Roman Catholic Church, and if you can show them from the Word of God how to find it, they come very easily, and make some of the best Christians. Always be sure of one thing, do not attack the Roman Catholic Church. This only awakens their prejudice and puts them in a bad position to be helped. Simply give them the truth, and the errors in time will take care of themselves. Not infrequently our attacks upon the Roman Catholic Church only expose our ignorance for oftentimes they do not believe just what we suppose they do. It is frequently desirable to use a Roman Catholic Bible in dealing with a Roman Catholic. Of course if one is going to do that, he should study up the texts beforehand in that version. Very many of the texts are for all practical purposes the same in the Roman Catholic version of the

Bible as in our own. One of the chief differences is that they trans-late "repent," "do penance."

II. Jews.

A great many Jews to-day are inquiring into the claims of Jesus the Nazarene, and are open to approach upon this subject. The best way to deal with a Jew is to show him that his own Bible points to Jesus as the Christ. Among the most useful passages for this purpose are Is. 53 (the entire chapter).

> "And after threescore and two weeks shall Messiah be cut off, but not for himself: and the people of the prince that shall come shall destroy the city and the sanctuary; and the end thereof shall be with a flood, and unto the end of the war desolations are determined." Dan. 9:26.
> "And I will pour upon the house of David, and upon the inhabitants of Jerusalem, the spirit of grace and of supplications: and they shall look upon me whom they have pierced, and they shall mourn for him, as one mourneth for his only Son, and shall be in bitterness for him, as one that is in bitterness for his firstborn." Zech. 12:10.
> "But thou, Bethlehem Ephratah, though thou be little among the thousands of Judah, yet out of thee shall he come forth unto me that is to be ruler in Israel; whose goings forth have been from of old, from everlasting." Micah 5:2.

If the Jew objects that these passages are different in his Hebrew Bible, do not allow yourself to be put off in this way, for they are not. He may say that Is. 53 does not refer to the Messiah. In that case ask him to whom it does refer. If he is a well-posted Jewish controversialist, very likely he will say, to suffering Israel. If he does say so, go through the chapter and show that it cannot refer to suffering Israel, because the one who suffers is plainly suffering for the sins of another, Is. 53:4, 5, and 8, and the other for whom he is suffering is God's people Israel, so of course the sufferer cannot himself be Israel.

The whole book of Hebrews is excellent to use with a Jew, especially the ninth and tenth chapters, and the seventh chapter, the 25th to the 28th verses.

The great difficulty in the way of the Jew coming out as a Christian, is the terrific persecution which he must endure if he does. Undoubtedly it costs a great deal to-day for a Jew to become a Christian, but if he brings up this question as he undoubtedly will, show him the passages already given under the head of those who are afraid of persecution, Chapter VII, Sec. XII.

There are a number of good tracts prepared especially for Jews which can be had from various missions to Jews in London, New York, Chicago, and other large centers of population.

III. Spiritualists.

Many people who call themselves Spiritualists claim to believe in the Bible. Such persons make a great deal of Samuel's appearing to Saul, I Sam. 28:11–20. It is not necessary to deny that Samuel really appeared to Saul, but show the one with whom you are dealing what the result was to Saul of thus consulting one who had a familiar spirit.

A good passage to use in dealing with all Spiritualists is I Chron. 10:13, 14:

> "So Saul died for his transgression which he committed against the Lord, even against the word of the Lord, which he kept not, and also *for asking counsel of one that had a familiar spirit*, to inquire of it; and inquired not of the Lord: therefore he slew him, and turned the kingdom unto David the son of Jesse."

Another excellent passage is Is. 8:19, 20:

> "And when they shall say unto you, *Seek unto them that have familiar spirits*, and unto wizards that peep, and that mutter: should not a people seek unto their God? for the living to the dead? *To the law and to the testimony:* if they speak not according to this word, it is because *there is no light in them.*"

I Jno. 4:1–3 is also a useful passage, as it brings out how not all spirits are to be believed. II Thess. 2:9–12 is also useful. All these passages can be followed up by:

> "Regard not them that have familiar spirits, neither seek after wizards, to be defiled by them: I am the Lord your God." Lev. 19:31.
> "And the soul that turneth after such as have familiar spirits, and after wizards, to go a whoring after them, I will even set my face against that soul, and will cut him off from among his people." Lev. 20:6.
> "There shall not be found among you any one that maketh his son or his daughter to pass through the fire, or that useth divination, or an observer of times, or an enchanter, or a witch, or a charmer, *or a consulter with familiar spirits*, or a wizard, or a necromancer. For all that do these things are an abomination unto the Lord: and because of these abominations the Lord thy God doth drive them out from before thee." Deut. 18:10–12.
> "Manasseh was twelve years old when he began to reign, and reigned fifty and five years in Jerusalem. And his mother's name was Hephzibah.

And he did that which was evil in the sight of the Lord after the abominations of the heathen, whom the Lord cast out before the children of Israel.

"And he made his son pass through the fire, and observed times, and used enchantments, *and dealt with familiar spirits and wizards:* he wrought much wickedness in the sight of the Lord, to provoke him to anger." II Kings 21:1, 2, 6.

These passages all show how God regards consulting spiritualists and mediums.

IV. Christian Scientists.

Many people in our day are being led astray into Christian Science, and we need to be ready to help them. Most Christian Scientists claim to believe the Bible. Take them to I Jno. 4:1–3:

"Beloved, believe not every spirit but try the spirits whether they are of God: because many false prophets are gone out into the world. Hereby know ye the Spirit of God: every spirit that *confesseth that Jesus Christ is come in the flesh* is of God: and *every spirit that confesseth not that Jesus Christ is come in the flesh is not of God:* and this is that spirit of antichrist, whereof ye have heard that it should come; and even now already is it in the world."

This passage strikes at the very foundation of Christian Science. Christian Science denies as one of its fundamental postulates, the reality of matter, and the reality of the body, and of necessity the reality of the incarnation. Show them by this passage that the Bible declares that every spirit that confesses not Jesus Christ *come in the flesh,* is not of God, but is the spirit of antichrist. Christian Science also denies the doctrine of substitution. Of course many Christian Scientists are not aware of this fact, for it is the common practice in leading one into Christian Science, not to let him see at once, all that is involved in it. Therefore take the one with whom you are dealing to such passages as the following:

"For he hath made him to be sin for us, who knew no sin; that we might be made the righteousness of God in him." II Cor. 5:21.

"Christ hath redeemed us from the curse of the law, *being made a curse for us:* for it is written, Cursed is every one that hangeth on a tree." Gal. 3:13.

"Who his own self bare our sins in his own body on the tree, that we, being dead to sins, should live unto righteousness: by whose stripes ye were healed." I Pet. 2:24.

> "And almost all things are by the law purged with blood; and *without shedding of blood* is no remission." Heb. 9:22.

In these passages the doctrine of substitution is clearly brought out.

The average Christian Scientist in defending his position, makes a great deal of the fact that the Christian Scientists have physical cures. Of this there can be no question. Many people are better physically because of Christian Science treatment, so it is neither necessary nor wise to deny the reality of all their cures. Admit the cure, and then show that the fact that one cures sickness proves nothing for the truth of the position he holds, or for his acceptance before God. Use for this purpose the following passages:

> "Many will say to me in that day, Lord, Lord, have we not prophesied in thy name? and in thy name have cast out devils? and in thy name done many wonderful works? And then will I profess unto them, I never knew you: depart from me, ye that work iniquity." Matt. 7:22, 23.
>
> "And then shall that Wicked be revealed, whom the Lord shall consume with the spirit of his mouth, and shall destroy with the brightness of his coming: even him, whose coming is *after the working of Satan with all power and signs and lying wonders.*" II Thess. 2:8, 9.
>
> "And no marvel; for Satan himself is transformed into an angel of light. Therefore it is no great thing if his ministers also be transformed as the ministers of righteousness; whose end shall be according to their works." II Cor. 11:14, 15.

V. Followers of false prophets.

New false prophets are constantly rising, and it is impossible to mention them all by name, furthermore they oftentimes disappear as rapidly as they appear, but practically the same method of treatment will serve to help.

1. First show the deluded one Christ's own warning that false Christs and false prophets would arise. For this purpose use Mark 13:22, 23:

> "For false Christs and false prophets shall rise, and shall shew signs and wonders, to seduce, if it were possible, even the elect. But take ye heed: behold, I have foretold you all things."

Dwell upon the point that the fact that they heal the sick and perform other wonders is no proof at all that they are not false prophets, that Christ distinctly foretold that the false Christs and the false prophets would do these things.

2. Then give them the following five rules by which they can escape every snare of the false prophet.

(1) The first rule is found in Jno. 7:17, *a will wholly surrendered to God.*

"If any man will do his will, he shall know of the doctrine, whether it be of God, or whether I speak of myself."

Make this point very clear, for many of these people claim to have wholly surrendered their wills to God, but question them unsparingly on this point, and oftentimes you will find that the will is not surrendered.

(2) The second rule is found in II Tim. 3:13–17. This rule is *a careful study of the Word of God, and a thorough comparison of any one's claims to be a prophet, or a Christ, or the Messenger of the Covenant, or John the Baptist, or anything of that sort, with the teachings of the Word of God.* The followers of false prophets generally make a hobby of some few verses in the Bible, and do not study the book as a whole.

(3) The third rule is found in James 1:5–7, *prayer to God for wisdom.*

"If any of you lack wisdom, let him ask of God, that giveth to all men liberally, and upbraideth not; and it shall be given him. But let him ask in faith, nothing wavering. For he that wavereth is like a wave of the sea driven with the wind and tossed. For let not that man think that he shall receive anything of the Lord."

Of course the prayer must be sincere, with a readiness to follow the leading of God. Many pray for guidance and still go on in delusion, but the prayer is not sincere. They ask for guidance, but do not utterly renounce their own wisdom and wait upon God for His wisdom. Very many have been led out of the error of following various false prophets when they in utter self-distrust have gone to God for light and guidance.

(4) The fourth rule is found in Matt. 23:8–10, *call no man master.*

"But be not ye called Rabbi: for one is your Master, even Christ; and all ye are brethren. And call no man your father upon the earth: for one is your Father, which is in heaven. Neither be ye called masters: for one is your Master, even Christ."

Call no man Master, acknowledge no man as an absolute and final authority, accept the authority of no one, and nothing but Christ and the Bible, in matters of faith and religion. It is well to dwell upon this point, for this is the very point at which many are led astray, the swallowing of some man whole, with all his arrant pretensions. The natural, selfish heart of man craves some man to do our thinking for us in matters of religion, and this makes men ready to swallow whole the teachings of some man. It is this that gives power to popery, priestcraft, Christian Science, Mormonism, and all similar delusions.

(5) The fifth rule is found in Prov. 29:25, *Be afraid of no man.*

"The fear of man bringeth a snare: but whoso putteth his trust in the Lord shall be safe."

Many a false prophet keeps his power over people through fear. While they do not more than half believe in him, they are afraid if they leave he will in some way bring sickness or some other curse upon them. Very likely the one with whom you are dealing will be in this very position. Show them how clearly they are in a wrong position, the very fact that they are afraid of the man proving this. Show the deluded man that the Holy Spirit is "not a spirit of fear, but of power, and of love, and of a sound mind." If the deluded person insists that the false prophet does his work in the name of Christ and succeeds, and therefore must be accepted of God, turn him to Matt. 7:22, 23. This shows very clearly that one may even cast out devils in the name of the Lord, and yet be one whom He never knew.

It is well in dealing with those who are under the spell of a false prophet to be able to show them what the marks of a false prophet are. The first and most common of these is a greed for money. To show this, use Titus 1:10, 11, and II Pet. 2:3:

"For there are many unruly and vain talkers and deceivers, specially they of the circumcision: whose mouths must be stopped, who subvert whole houses, teaching things which they ought not, *for filthy lucre's sake.*"

"And *through covetousness* shall they with feigned words make merchandise of you: whose judgment now of a long time lingereth not, and their damnation slumbereth not."

Make it very clear if the pretended prophet is trying to get money from the people (as usually he very clearly is), that that in itself is a mark that he is a false prophet. A second mark of the false prophet is vaunting one's self. To show the deluded one this, use Jude 16 and I Cor. 13:4, R. V.:

"These are murmurers, complainers, walking after their own lusts; and *their mouth speaketh great swelling words,* having men's persons in admiration because of advantage."

"Love suffereth long, and is kind; love envieth not; love vaunteth not itself, is not puffed up."

A third mark of the false prophet is the claim to an authority that Jesus Christ forbade any man ascribing to himself. To show this to some person who is in the snare of the false prophet use Matt. 23:8, 12. A fourth mark of a false prophet is a false application of Scripture either to himself, or to places with which he is connected. Thus, for example, the Mormons take passages which apply to Israel, and apply them to their own Zion. When any place under the false prophet's control is named for some Bible place, and Scriptural promises referring to the literal Bible place are applied to the place under the prophet's control, just show the one who is being deceived by this sort of thing how utterly unwarranted such an application is. Fifth, there is usually an untrue note somewhere in the doctrine taught by the false prophet. He may teach a good deal that is Biblical and true, but somewhere he betrays his Satanic origin. The points at which this false note of doctrine are most likely to be found are on the doctrine of future punishment, the matter of the use of meats, or upon legalism of some form—the observation of the seventh day, the matter of tithes, or something of that sort. In the matter of future punishment, false prophets generally go off sooner or later into either annihilationism or restorationism or a combination of the two.

After all the most important thing to do in dealing with one who is under a delusion, is to bring forward the fundamental, saving truth of the Gospel, salvation through the atoning work and upon the single condition of faith in Jesus Christ. Oftentimes error, like typhoid fever, has to be left to take its course and work itself out. I know many men to-day who are out in a clear Christian experience, who for a while were completely under the control of some of our modern false prophets, even thinking that all who did not agree with them were utterly wrong, and saying so in the most bitter terms; but in answer to prayer, and the study of the Word of God, God has led them out of the darkness into the light.

CHAPTER XIV

HOW TO DEAL WITH CHRISTIANS WHO NEED COUNSEL, REBUKE, ENCOURAGEMENT, OR COMFORT

It is often necessary to do personal work with those who are really Christians, but whose Christian experience for one cause or another is unsatisfactory.

I. Christians who are neglecting the open confession of Christ.

There are many who are professing Christians who are not making an open confession of Christ as they ought. The experience of such is of course always unsatisfactory. No one can make satisfactory progress in the Christian life who is not confessing Christ openly before men. One of the best passages of Scripture to use with this class is Matt. 10:32, 33:

"*Whosoever therefore shall confess me before men*, him will I confess also before my Father which is in heaven. But whosoever shall deny me before men, him will I also deny before my Father which is in heaven."

The meaning and application of this verse is so plain as to need no comment.

Another excellent passage to use is Rom. 10:9, 10:

"*If thou shalt confess with thy mouth* the Lord Jesus, and shalt believe in thine heart that God hath raised him from the dead, thou shalt be saved. For with the heart man believeth unto righteousness; and *with the mouth confession is made unto salvation*."

According to this passage, our very salvation depends upon the confession of Jesus Christ with the mouth. There are many who say that they are Christians and who believe that they are saved, because in their hearts they believe in Jesus and have accepted Him as a Saviour. They will tell you that they do not regard a public confession of Christ as necessary. The passage just given will show them how utterly unscriptural is their position. A short time ago a man who called himself a Christian, and who entertained the hope that he really was a child of God, but who lacked joy in his experience, approached me with the question, "Do you think it is necessary that a man should publicly confess Christ in order to be saved?" I replied, "It is a matter of very little moment what I think is necessary, the great question is, what does God tell us in His own Word?" Then I gave him Rom. 10:9, 10 to read. "Now," I said, "that is what God says." The meaning and application of the passage were so plain that the man had nothing further to say, but promised to make an open confession of Christ before the world.

Another helpful passage to use is John 12:42, 43:

> "Nevertheless among the chief rulers also many believed on him; but because of the Pharisees they did not confess him, lest they should be put out of the synagogue: for they loved the praise of men more than the praise of God."

In many cases I have found that where these other passages did not seem to lead to decisive action, Mark 8:38 did:

> "Whosoever therefore shall be ashamed of me and of my words in this adulterous and sinful generation; of him also shall the Son of man be ashamed, when he cometh in the glory of his Father with the holy angels."

II. Christians who are neglecting the Bible.

There are many to-day who make a profession of faith in Jesus Christ, and of whom doubtless many are saved, who are making little or no progress in the Christian life because of neglect of the Bible. A good passage to use with such is I Pet. 2:2:

> "As newborn babes, desire the sincere milk of the word, that ye may grow thereby."

I was once calling upon a member of the church. I put to her the question, "How are you getting along in your Christian life?" She replied, "I am not getting on at all; my Christian life is a disgrace to me, a disgrace to the church, and a disgrace to Jesus Christ."

I then asked, "Are you studying the Word of God daily?" She replied that she was not. "No wonder then that your Christian experience is not satisfactory," said I. A little baby was lying in a carriage close at hand. I pointed to the child and said, "Suppose that you fed this baby every two hours to-day, once every six hours to-morrow, not at all the next day, three or four times the next day, and then let her go two or three days without feeding at all, how do you think the baby would thrive?" She replied, "I do not think the baby would thrive at all, I think she would die." "Well," I said, "this is the exact way in which you are treating your soul." This point is emphasized by the passage just given.

Another passage to use with this class is Acts 20:32:

"And now, brethren, I commend you to God, and to the word of his grace, which is able to build you up, and to give you an inheritance among all them which are sanctified."

Other helpful passages are:

"Wherefore lay apart all filthiness and superfluity of naughtiness, and receive with meekness the engrafted word, which is able to save your souls. But be ye doers of the word, and not hearers only, deceiving your own selves." James 1:21, 22.

"But evil men and seducers shall wax worse and worse, deceiving and being deceived. But continue thou in the things which thou hast learned and hast been assured of, knowing of whom thou hast learned them; and that from a child thou hast known *the holy scriptures, which are able to make thee wise unto salvation* through faith which is in Christ Jesus. All scripture is given by inspiration of God, and is profitable for doctrine, for reproof, for correction, for instruction in righteousness: that the man of God may be perfect, thoroughly furnished unto all good works." II Tim. 3:13–17.

"And take the helmet of salvation, and the sword of the Spirit, which is the word of God." Eph. 6:17.

"Wherewithal shall a young man cleanse his way? By taking heed thereto *according to thy word.*

"Thy word have I hid in mine heart, that I might not sin against thee."

"The entrance of thy words giveth light; it giveth understanding unto the simple." Ps. 119:9, 11, 130.

"Blessed is the man that walketh not in the counsel of the ungodly, nor standeth in the way of sinners, nor sitteth in the seat of the scornful. But his delight is in the law of the LORD: and *in his law doth he meditate day and night.*" Ps. 1:1, 2.

In the use of the last passage especially emphasize the second verse, "His delight is in the law of the LORD; And in his law

doth he *meditate day and night.*" In a similar way you can use
Josh. 1:8:

> "This book of the law shall not depart out of thy mouth; but thou shalt
> *meditate therein day and night*, that thou mayest observe to do according
> to all that is written therein: for *then* thou shalt make thy way prosper-
> ous, and then thou shalt have good success."

A passage which is useful as emphasizing the need of *daily*
searching the Scriptures is Acts 17:11:

> "These were more noble than those in Thessalonica, in that they re-
> ceived the word with all readiness of mind, and searched the scriptures
> *daily*, whether those things were so."

In urging upon others the daily study of the Scriptures it is
always well to give them a few simple directions as to how to
study the Bible.

III. Christians who are neglecting prayer.

One of the commonest causes in our day of an unsatisfactory
Christian experience, is neglect of prayer. A personal worker will
often find those who complain that they are not making satisfactory progress in the Christian life. In such a case the worker should
always inquire whether they make a regular practice of prayer and
to what extent. When it is found that prayer is being neglected,
the following passages will be found useful:

> "Ye lust, and have not: ye kill, and desire to have, and cannot obtain:
> ye fight and war, yet ye have not, *because ye ask not.*" James 4:2.

In using this passage, emphasize the seven closing words:

> "And I say unto you, Ask, and it shall be given you; seek, and ye shall
> find; knock, and it shall be opened unto you. For every one that asketh
> receiveth; and he that seeketh findeth; and to him that knocketh it shall be
> opened. If a son shall ask bread of any of you that is a father, will he give
> him a stone? or if he ask a fish, will he for a fish give him a serpent? or
> if he shall ask an egg, will he offer him a scorpion? If ye then, being evil,
> know how to give good gifts unto your children: how much more shall
> your heavenly Father give the Holy Spirit *to them that ask him?*" Luke
> 11:9–13.
> "Is any among you afflicted? *let him pray.* Is any merry? let him sing
> psalms. Is any sick among you? let him call for the elders of the church;

and let them pray over him, anointing him with oil in the name of the Lord: And the prayer of faith shall save the sick, and the Lord shall raise him up; and if he have committed sins, they shall be forgiven him. Confess your faults one to another, and pray one for another, that ye may be healed. *The effectual fervent prayer of a righteous man availeth much.*

"Elias was a man subject to like passions as we are, and he prayed earnestly that it might not rain; and it rained not on the earth by the space of three years and six months. And he prayed again, and the heaven gave rain, and the earth brought forth her fruit." James 5:13–18.

"And said unto them, Why sleep ye? rise and *pray, lest ye enter into temptation.*" Luke 22:46.

The last passage is especially helpful as emphasizing one of the most important purposes of prayer. Another exceedingly instructive passage along this line is Is. 40:31:

"But *they that wait upon the Lord* shall renew their strength; they shall mount up with wings as eagles; they shall run, and not be weary; and they shall walk, and not faint."

A passage which is useful as suggesting the need of regular seasons of prayer is Ps. 55:17:

"Evening, and morning, and at noon, will I pray, and cry aloud: and he shall hear my voice."

Other passages which are useful in dealing with people of this class are:

"And in the morning, rising up a great while before day, he went out, and departed into a solitary place, and there prayed." Mark 1:35.

"Now when Daniel knew that the writing was signed, he went into his house; and his windows being open in his chamber toward Jerusalem, he kneeled upon his knees three times a day, and prayed, and gave thanks before his God, as he did aforetime." Dan. 6:10.

"And when he had sent them away, he departed into a mountain to pray." Mark 6:46.

"And it came to pass in those days, that he went out into a mountain to pray, and continued all night in prayer to God." Luke 6:12.

"*Pray without ceasing.*" I Thess. 5:17.

IV. Christians who are leading careless lives.

There are many whom one would hesitate to say are not Christians at all and are not saved, but whose lives are not out and out for Christ as they should be. In dealing with such, the following passages will be found particularly useful: II Cor. 6:14–7:1; especially emphasize in these verses, the words, "Come ye out from among them, and be ye separate."

"No man can serve two masters: for either he will hate the one, and love the other; or else he will hold to the one, and despise the other. *Ye cannot serve God and mammon.*" Matt. 6:24.

In the above passage, dwell upon and drive home the closing words, "Ye cannot serve God and mammon."

"*Love not the world,* neither the things that are in the world. If any man love the world, the love of the Father is not in him. For all that is in the world, the lust of the flesh, and the lust of the eyes, and the pride of life, is not of the Father, but is of the world. And the world passeth away, and the lust thereof: but he that doeth the will of God abideth forever." I John 2:15–17.

"Ye adulterers and adulteresses, know ye not that *the friendship of the world is enmity with God?* whosoever therefore shall be a friend of the world is the enemy of God.

"But he giveth more grace. Wherefore he saith, God resisteth the proud, but giveth grace unto the humble. Submit yourselves therefore to God. Resist the devil, and he will flee from you. Draw nigh to God, and he will draw nigh to you. Cleanse your hands, ye sinners; and purify your hearts, ye double minded." James 4:4, 6–8.

"Follow peace with all men, and holiness, without which no man shall see the Lord." Heb. 12:14.

"Wherefore gird up the loins of your mind, be sober, and hope to the end for the grace that is to be brought unto you at the revelation of Jesus Christ; as obedient children, not fashioning yourselves according to the former lusts in your ignorance: but as he which hath called you is holy, so be ye holy in all manner of conversation; because it is written, Be ye holy; for I am holy. And if ye call on the Father, who without respect of persons judgeth according to every man's work, pass the time of your sojourning here in fear: forasmuch as ye know that ye were not redeemed with corruptible things, as silver and gold, from your vain conversation received by tradition from your fathers; but with the precious blood of Christ, as of a lamb without blemish and without spot." I Peter 1:13–19.

"For the time is come that judgment must begin at the house of God: and if it first begin at us, what shall the end be of them that obey not the gospel of God? And if the righteous scarcely be saved, where shall the ungodly and the sinner appear?" I Peter 4:17, 18.

"And that which fell among thorns are they, which, when they have heard, go forth, and are *choked with cares and riches and pleasures of this life,* and bring no fruit to perfection." Luke 8:14.

In using the above passage, dwell upon the thought contained in the words, "choked with cares and riches and pleasures of this life."

"And take heed to yourselves, lest at any time your hearts be over-charged with surfeiting, and drunkenness, and cares of this life, and so that day come upon you unawares. For as a snare shall it come on all them that dwell on the face of the whole earth. Watch ye therefore, and pray always, that ye may be accounted worthy to escape all these things that shall come to pass, and to stand before the Son of man." Luke 21:34–36.

"Let your loins be girded about, and your lights burning; and ye your-selves like unto men that wait for their lord, when he will return from the wedding; that when he cometh and knocketh, they may open unto him immediately. Blessed are those servants, whom the lord when he cometh shall find watching; verily I say unto you, that he shall gird him-self, and make them to sit down to meat, and will come forth and serve them. And if he shall come in the second watch, or come in the third watch, and find them so, blessed are those servants." Luke 12:35–38.

"I beseech you therefore, brethren, by the mercies of God, that ye present your bodies a living sacrifice, holy, acceptable unto God, which is your reasonable service. And be not conformed to this world: but be ye transformed by the renewing of your mind, that ye may prove what is that good, and acceptable, and perfect, will of God." Rom. 12:1, 2.

"And he that doubteth is damned if he eat, because he eateth not of faith: for whatsoever is not of faith is sin." Rom. 14:23.

"I have fought a good fight, I have finished my course, I have kept the faith: henceforth there is laid up for me a crown of righteousness, which the Lord, the righteous judge, shall give me at that day: and not to me only, but unto all them also that love his appearing." II Tim. 4:7, 8.

V. Christians who are not working for Christ.

A large proportion of the professing church to-day is doing little or nothing for the Master. The personal worker who shall succeed in getting other Christians to work will be accomplishing at least as much for Christ as the one who leads the unsaved to Him. The Bible abounds in passages which can be effectively used for this purpose. The following will be found useful: Mark 13:34–37 (emphasize the words "to every man his work"); Matt. 24: 44–51 and Matt. 25:14–30. A verse which is useful in showing idle Christians that every professed follower of Christ ought to be a witness for Him and a soul winner is Acts 8:4:

"Therefore they that were scattered abroad went everywhere preaching the word."

Eph. 4:14–16 is also useful:

"That we henceforth be no more children, tossed to and fro, and car-ried about with every wind of doctrine, by the sleight of men, and cunning craftiness, whereby they lie in wait to deceive; but speaking the truth in love, may grow up into him in all things, which is the head, even Christ:

from whom the whole body fitly joined together and compacted *by that which every joint supplieth,* according to the effectual working in the measure of every part, maketh increase of the body unto the edifying of itself in love."

In using this passage, point out the words, "that which every joint supplieth," and explain their meaning. Other verses that will be found useful are Eph. 5:14–21:

"She hath done what she could." Mark 14:8.

"Let him know, that he which converteth the sinner from the error of his way shall save a soul from death, and shall hide a multitude of sins." James 5:20.

"And they that be wise shall shine as the brightness of the firmament; and they that turn many to righteousness as the stars for ever and ever." Dan. 12:3.

"And, behold, I come quickly; and my reward is with me, *to give every man according as his work shall be.*" Rev. 22:12.

VI. Christians who are undergoing temptation.

There come to all Christians, and especially to all young Christians, times of special temptation and trial. At such times they need, and should have, the counsel and encouragement of other Christians. We should bear one another's burdens, and so fulfill the law of Christ. (Gal. 6:2.) Here is a large field of usefulness for the personal worker. The following passages will be found exceedingly useful in strengthening the brethren when under trial and temptation.

"My brethren, count it all joy when ye fall into divers temptations; knowing this, that the trying of your faith worketh patience. But let patience have her perfect work, that ye may be perfect and entire, wanting nothing." James 1:2–4.

"Blessed is the man that endureth temptation: for when he is tried, he shall receive the crown of life, which the Lord hath promised to them that love him." James 1:12.

"Be sober, be vigilant; because your adversary the devil, as a roaring lion, walketh about, seeking whom he may devour: whom resist stedfast in the faith, knowing that the same afflictions are accomplished in your brethren that are in the world. But the God of all grace, who hath called us unto his eternal glory by Christ Jesus, after that ye have suffered a while, make you perfect, stablish, strengthen, settle you." I Pet. 5:8–10.

(It is well when possible to use the R. V. of the last passage.)

"There hath no temptation taken you but such as is common to man: but God is faithful, who will not suffer you to be tempted above that ye are able; but will with the temptation also make a way to escape, that ye may be able to bear it." I Cor. 10:13.

"And he said unto me, My grace is sufficient for thee: for my strength is made perfect in weakness. Most gladly therefore will I rather glory in my infirmities, that the power of Christ may rest upon me. Therefore I take pleasure in infirmities, in reproaches, in necessities, in persecutions, in distresses for Christ's sake: for when I am weak, then am I strong." II Cor. 12:9, 10.

"Pray without ceasing." I Thess. 5:17.

"I can do all things through Christ which strengtheneth me." Phil. 4:13.

"I have written unto you, fathers, because ye have known him that is from the beginning. I have written unto you, young men, because ye are strong, and the word of God abideth in you, and ye have overcome the wicked one." I Jno. 2:14.

"Wherewithal shall a young man cleanse his way? By taking heed thereto according to thy word." Ps. 119:9.

"He giveth power to the faint; and to them that have no might he increaseth strength. Even the youths shall faint and be weary, and the young men shall utterly fall: but they that wait upon the LORD shall renew their strength; they shall mount up with wings as eagles; they shall run, and not be weary; and they shall walk, and not faint." Is. 40:29–31.

VII. Christians who are undergoing persecution.

Many professed Christians fail in the hour of persecution who would have stood if they could have had a few words of counsel from some fellow Christian. The following passages are useful in giving the needed word of counsel and encouragement:

"Blessed are they which are persecuted for righteousness' sake: for theirs is the kingdom of heaven. Blessed are ye, when men shall revile you, and persecute you, and shall say all manner of evil against you falsely, for my sake. Rejoice, and be exceeding glad: for great is your reward in heaven: for so persecuted they the prophets which were before you." Matt. 5:10–12.

"Beloved, think it not strange concerning the fiery trial which is to try you, as though some strange thing happened unto you: but rejoice, inasmuch as ye are partakers of Christ's sufferings; that, when his glory shall be revealed, ye may be glad also with exceeding joy. If ye be reproached for the name of Christ, happy are ye; for the spirit of glory and of God resteth upon you: on their part he is evil spoken of, but on your part he is glorified." I Pet. 4:12–14.

"Yet if any man suffer as a Christian, let him not be ashamed; but let him glorify God on this behalf." I Pet. 4:16.

"For even hereunto were ye called: because Christ also suffered for us, leaving us an example, that ye should follow his steps: who did no sin, neither was guile found in his mouth: who, when he was reviled, reviled not again; when he suffered, he threatened not; but committed himself to him that judgeth righteously." I Pet. 2:21–23.

"For it is better, if the will of God be so, that ye suffer for well doing, than for evil doing. For Christ also hath once suffered for sins, the just for the unjust, that he might bring us to God, being put to death in the flesh, but quickened by the Spirit." I Pet. 3:17, 18.

"Yea, and all that will live godly in Christ Jesus shall suffer persecution." II Tim. 3:12.

"Confirming the souls of the disciples, and exhorting them to continue in the faith, and that we must through much tribulation enter into the kingdom of God." Acts 14:22.

"And to him they agreed: and when they had called the apostles, and beaten them, they commanded that they should not speak in the name of Jesus, and let them go. And they departed from the presence of the council, rejoicing that they were counted worthy to suffer shame for his name.

"And daily in the temple, and in every house, they ceased not to teach and preach Jesus Christ." Acts 5:40–42.

"Wherefore seeing we also are compassed about with so great a cloud of witnesses, let us lay aside every weight, and the sin which doth so easily beset us, and let us run with patience the race that is set before us, looking unto Jesus the author and finisher of our faith; who for the joy that was set before him endured the cross, despising the shame, and is set down at the right hand of the throne of God. For consider him that endured such contradiction of sinners against himself, lest ye be wearied and faint in your minds. Ye have not yet resisted unto blood, striving against sin." Heb. 12:1–4.

"Fear none of those things which thou shalt suffer: behold, the devil shall cast some of you into prison, that ye may be tried; and ye shall have tribulation ten days: be thou faithful unto death, and I will give thee a crown of life." Rev. 2:10.

"Fear not, little flock; for it is your Father's good pleasure to give you the kingdom." Luke 12:32.

VIII. Christians who are passing through affliction.

When times of affliction come to Christians, especially to young Christians, a few words fitly spoken by a fellow Christian are oftentimes of great help. Not infrequently they save the afflicted one from years of darkness and barrenness in their Christian experience. There are many to-day who are of little or no use in the church, who would have been of use if some wise worker had come to them in the hour of affliction and given them good counsel from God's own Word. We should all be constantly on the lookout for opportunities of this kind, and we will find them round about us almost every day of our lives. No thoughts of our own can possibly be of as much help in such an hour as the promises and encouragements of God's Word. The following passages will be found useful and sufficient, if wisely used in the power of the Holy Spirit:

"And ye have forgotten the exhortation which speaketh unto you as unto children, My son, despise not thou the chastening of the Lord, nor faint when thou art rebuked of him: for whom the Lord loveth he chasteneth, and scourgeth every son whom he receiveth. If ye endure chastening, God dealeth with you as with sons; for what son is he whom the father chasteneth not?"

"Now no chastening for the present seemeth to be joyous, but grievous: nevertheless afterward it yieldeth the peaceable fruit of righteousness unto them which are exercised thereby." Heb. 12:5–7, 11.

"To an inheritance incorruptible, and undefiled, and that fadeth not away, reserved in heaven for you, who are kept by the power of God through faith unto salvation ready to be revealed in the last time. Wherein ye greatly rejoice, though now for a season, if need be, ye are in heaviness through manifold temptations: that the trial of your faith, being much more precious than of gold that perisheth, though it be tried with fire, might be found unto praise and honour and glory at the appearing of Jesus Christ." I Pet. 1:4–7.

"Humble yourselves therefore under the mighty hand of God, that he may exalt you in due time: casting all your care upon him; for he careth for you." I Pet. 5:6, 7.

"God is our refuge and strength, *a very present help in trouble*. Therefore will not we fear, though the earth be removed, and though the mountains be carried into the midst of the sea; though the waters thereof roar and be troubled, though the mountains shake with the swelling thereof." Ps. 46:1–3.

"Yea, though I walk through the valley of the shadow of death,, I will fear no evil: for thou art with me; thy rod and thy staff they comfort me." Ps. 23:4.

"And call upon me in the day of trouble: I will deliver thee, and thou shalt glorify me." Ps. 50:15.

"The righteous cry, and the LORD heareth, and delivereth them out of all their troubles." Ps. 34:17.

"The LORD is my light and my salvation; Whom shall I fear? the LORD is the strength of my life; of whom shall I be afraid? When the wicked, even mine enemies and my foes, came upon me to eat up my flesh, they stumbled and fell. Though an host should encamp against me, my heart shall not fear: though war should rise against me in this will I be confident. One thing have I desired of the LORD, that will I seek after; that I may dwell in the house of the LORD all the days of my life, to behold the beauty of the LORD, and to enquire in his temple. For *in the time of trouble he shall hide me in his pavilion:* in the secret of his tabernacle shall he hide me; he shall set me upon a rock. And now shall mine head be lifted up above mine enemies round about me: therefore will I offer in his tabernacle sacrifices of joy; I will sing, yea, I will sing praises unto the Lord.

"I had fainted, unless I had believed to see the goodness of the LORD in the land of the living. Wait on the LORD: be of good courage, and he shall strengthen thine heart: wait, I say, on the LORD." Ps. 27:1–6, 13, 14.

"Come unto me, all ye that labour and are heavy laden, and I will give you rest. Take my yoke upon you, and learn of me; for I am meek and lowly in heart: and ye shall find rest unto your souls." Matt. 11:28, 29.

The one who is to use these passages should first read them over and over again with himself alone, and think of their relation to the specific trial of the one whom he proposes to help.

IX. Christians who have lost loved ones.

The ministry of comfort to those whose homes have been invaded by death is one of the most blessed of Christian ministries. It is a ministry that is open to us all, but the attempts of many well-meaning persons in this direction, who try to comfort with their own fancies rather than with the sure Word of God, oftentimes do more harm than good. But the one who knows his Bible, and what it has to say upon the subject of death and of the future, will be able to bind up many a broken heart. Jesus declared in the synagogue at Nazareth, that God had anointed Him to heal the broken hearted, (Luke 4:18), and every follower of Jesus should seek an anointing for the same blessed work. The Bible abounds in passages which are useful for this purpose, but the following are among those which experience proves to be most effective:

"Let not your heart be troubled: ye believe in God, believe also in me. In my Father's house are many mansions: if it were not so, I would have told you. I go to prepare a place for you. And if I go and prepare a place for you, I will come again, and receive you unto myself, that where I am, there ye may be also.

"Peace I leave with you, my peace I give unto you: not as the world giveth, give I unto you. Let not your heart be troubled, neither let it be afraid." Jno. 14:1–3, 27.

"Jesus answered and said unto him, What I do thou knowest not now; but thou shalt know hereafter." Jno. 13:7.

"Be still, and know that I am God: I will be exalted among the heathen, I will be exalted in the earth." Ps. 46:10.

"And I heard a voice from heaven saying unto me, Write, Blessed are the dead which die in the Lord from henceforth: Yea, saith the Spirit, that they may rest from their labours; and their works do follow them." Rev. 14:13.

"And he said, While the child was yet alive, I fasted and wept; for I said, Who can tell whether GOD will be gracious to me, that the child may live? But now he is dead, wherefore should I fast? Can I bring him back again? I shall go to him, but he shall not return to me." II Sam. 12:22, 23.

"But I would not have you to be ignorant, brethren, concerning them which are asleep, that ye sorrow not, even as others which have no hope. For if we believe that Jesus died and rose again, even so them also which sleep in Jesus will God bring with him. For this we say unto you by the word of the Lord, that we which are alive and remain unto the coming of the Lord shall not prevent them which are asleep. For the Lord himself shall descend from heaven with a shout, with the voice of the archangel, and with the trump of God: and the dead in Christ shall rise first: then we which are alive and remain shall be caught up together with them in the clouds, to meet the Lord in the air: and so shall we ever be with the Lord. Wherefore comfort one another with these words. " I Thess. 4:13–18.

(I have found this the most comforting of any single passage in the Word of God.)

"Therefore we are always confident, knowing that, whilst we are at home in the body, we are absent from the Lord: (for we walk by faith, not by sight:) we are confident, I say, and willing rather to be absent from the body, and to be present with the Lord." II Cor. 5:6–8.

"I am in a strait betwixt two, having a desire to depart, and to be with Christ; which is far better." Phil. 1:23.

"So also is the resurrection of the dead. It is sown in corruption, it is raised in incorruption: it is sown in dishonour, it is raised in glory: it is sown in weakness, it is raised in power: it is sown a natural body, it is raised a spiritual body. There is a natural body, and there is a spiritual body.

"And as we have borne the image of the earthy, we shall also bear the image of the heavenly.

"For this corruptible must put on incorruption, and this mortal must put on immortality.

"So when this corruptible shall have put on incorruption, and this mortal shall have put on immortality, then shall be brought to pass the saying that is written, Death is swallowed up in victory. O death, where is thy sting? O grave, where is thy victory? The sting of death is sin; and the strength of sin is the law. But thanks be to God, which giveth us the victory through our Lord Jesus Christ. Therefore, my beloved brethren, be ye stedfast, unmoveable, always abounding in the work of the Lord, forasmuch as ye know that your labour is not in vain in the Lord." I Cor. 15:42–44, 49, 53, 54–58.

The worker must make a study of each individual case, and decide which of the passages given above will be most helpful in the specific case. Sometimes it will be found well to use them all. They should not be merely read, but dwelt upon, and their meaning explained and applied, wherever necessary. In all the reading and the explanation and the application, we must depend upon the Holy Spirit for His wisdom and power.

X. Christians who have not received the Holy Spirit.

There are many professing Christians in our day who have not definitely received the Holy Spirit. They have not entered into the fulness of joy and peace and power that there is for us in Christ. They are practically in the same condition that the disciples in Ephesus were in until Paul came and put to them the question, "Have ye received the Holy Ghost?" (Acts 19:2) and the position that the believers in Samaria were in until Peter and John came down and "prayed for them, that they might receive the Holy Ghost: for as yet he was fallen upon none of them," (Acts 8: 15, 16). There are many to-day who are inquiring what they must do that they may receive the Holy Ghost, and there are others that ought to be asking this question. The personal worker should know how to show any one who has not received the Holy Spirit just what he must do that he may receive the Holy Spirit. The following are the steps that should be pointed out:

1. *The one who would receive the Holy Ghost must depend for his acceptance before God upon the finished work of Christ alone, and not upon anything he himself has done or can do.* To make this point clear to the inquirer use Gal. 3:2:

"This only would I learn of you, *Received ye the Spirit by the works of the law, or by hearing of faith?*"

This passage is often interpreted to mean that we receive the Holy Spirit by simply believing that we are going to receive Him. This is not at all the meaning of the passage as found in the context. The Christians in Galatia had been told by certain false teachers that came in among them, that in order to be justified it was not enough to simply believe on Jesus Christ and His finished work, but in addition to this they must keep the Mosaic law regarding circumcision. Paul in the passage before us shows them the folly of this position by appealing to their own experience. He calls to mind the fact that they had received the Holy Ghost not by keeping the Mosaic law, but simply by the hearing of faith, that is by believing God's testimony regarding Christ and His atoning work, and resting in that for pardon.

The first step then, toward receiving the Holy Spirit is to turn our eyes entirely away from ourselves, and anything we ever have done or can do, and fix them upon Jesus Christ, and His atoning work on the Cross, and depend upon that finished work of Christ for our pardon and acceptance before God.

2. *The one who would receive the Holy Ghost must put away all sin.* To make this clear to the inquirer use Acts 2:38:

> "Then Peter said unto them, *Repent,* and be baptized every one of you in the name of Jesus Christ for the remission of sins, and *ye shall receive the gift of the Holy Ghost.*"

This passage makes it clear that in order to receive the Holy Ghost we must repent. Repentance is a change of mind about Christ and a change of mind about sin. It is a change first of all from a Christ-rejecting attitude of mind, to a Christ-accepting attitude of mind. This is involved in what has been already said regarding the first step, but there must also be a change of mind regarding sin; a change of mind from a sin-loving and sin-indulging attitude of mind to a sin-rejecting attitude of mind, that is, we must renounce all sin. One of the commonest hindrances to the receiving of the Holy Spirit is holding on to some sin. The worker should deal very faithfully at this point with the inquirer. Find out whether there is not some sin in the life that is not renounced. Find if there is not some sin in the past that has not been confessed and straightened out. Instruct the inquirer to go alone with God and ask God to search his heart, and to show him anything in his life that is displeasing to Him. If anything is thus brought to light, insist that it must be renounced. Tell the inquirer that every known sin must be given up. Dwell upon the fact that the Holy Spirit is the *holy* Spirit, and that He will not manifest Himself in His fulness in an unholy heart, that is in a heart which holds on to sin.

3. *The one who would receive the Holy Spirit must surrender his will absolutely to the will of God.* To show this use Acts 5:32:

> "And we are his witnesses of these things; and so is also the Holy Ghost, whom God hath given *to them that obey him.*"

This passage shows that God gives the Holy Spirit to them that obey Him. Show that the essential thing about obedience is the attitude of the will, and that real obedience involves the absolute surrender of the will to God. Hold the inquirer to the necessity of such an absolute surrender to God. This is the point of difficulty in very many lives. Perhaps more people are kept out of the blessing of the conscious receiving of the Holy Spirit by a lack of absolute surrender than by any other one thing. In many an instance the Holy Spirit is given at once in fulness as soon as one is led to an absolute surrender of the will to God. If one will not thus surrender, there is no use of trying to go further, God will accept no compromise at this point.

4. *The one who would receive the Holy Spirit should ask God for this definite gift.* To show this to the inquirer use Luke 11:13:

> "If ye then, being evil, know how to give good gifts unto your children: how much more shall your heavenly Father give the Holy Spirit *to them that ask him?*"

This tells us plainly that God gives the Holy Spirit to them that ask Him. It can be illustrated by the use of Acts 2:1–4, cf. Acts 1:14; Acts 4:31 and Acts 8:15, 16:

> "And when the day of Pentecost was fully come, they were all with one accord in one place. And suddenly there came a sound from heaven as of a rushing mighty wind, and it filled all the house where they were sitting. And there appeared unto them cloven tongues like as of fire, and it sat upon each of them. And they were *all filled with the Holy Ghost,* and began to speak with other tongues, as the Spirit gave them utterance." Acts 2:1–4. (Compare Acts 1:14. "These all *continued with one accord in prayer* and supplication, with the women, and Mary the mother of Jesus, and with his brethren.")
>
> "And *when they had prayed,* the place was shaken where they were assembled together; and they were *all filled with the Holy Ghost,* and they spake the word of God with boldness." Acts 4:31.
>
> "Who, when they were come down, *prayed for them,* that they might receive the Holy Ghost: (for as yet he was fallen upon none of them: only they were baptized in the name of the Lord Jesus)." Acts 8:15, 16.

The inquirer should be led to at once definitely seek the filling with the Holy Spirit. It is well to pray with the inquirer then and there for this definite gift.

5. *The final step in receiving the Holy Ghost is simply faith.* There are many who take all the steps mentioned thus far, and yet fail of the blessing simply because they do not believe. Mark 11:24 can be used to make this clear:

> "Therefore I say unto you, What things soever ye desire, when ye pray, *believe that ye receive them,* and ye shall have them."

The R. V. of this passage is particularly suggestive.

"All things whatsoever ye pray and ask for, *believe that ye have received them,* and ye shall have them."

The inquirer should be instructed not to look to his feelings, but to the Word of God, and to believe that he has received whether he has any sensation or experience or not, simply because God has promised in His Word. In a very large proportion of cases, people receive the Holy Ghost simply by believing God's Word, and that their prayer is heard, without any feeling; and afterwards what they believe they "have received" they do actually obtain in personal experience as a conscious possession. Great help will be found in showing the inquirer how to receive by faith, in I Jno. 5:14, 15:

"And this is the confidence that we have in him, that, *if we ask anything according to his will, he heareth us:* and if we know that he hear us, whatsoever we ask, *we know that we have the petitions that we desired of him.*"

Make it very clear to the inquirer by the use of this passage that when we ask anything according to the will of God, we know that He heareth us, because the passage says so, and when we know that He heareth us, we know that we have the petitions we have asked of Him, *whether we feel it or not.*

Then show the inquirer that when we pray for the Holy Spirit we pray for something according to the will of God. The following passages make this clear:

"If ye then, being evil, know how to give good gifts unto your children: how much more shall your heavenly Father give the Holy Spirit to them that ask him?" Luke 11:13.

"Then Peter said unto them, Repent, and be baptized every one of you in the name of Jesus Christ for the remission of sins, and ye shall receive the gift of the Holy Ghost. For the promise is unto you, and to your children, and to all that are afar off, even as many as the Lord our God shall call." Acts 2:38, 39.

"And be not drunk with wine, wherein is excess, but *be filled with the Spirit.*" Eph. 5:18.

Then have the inquirer kneel down and definitely pray for the Holy Spirit. When he has offered this prayer, ask him if he has received what he sought. If he is not clear about it, open your Bible to I Jno. 5:14, 15 and lay it before him and have him read

it, and then ask him if he has asked for something according to
God's will, and when he says he has, ask him, "What then do you
know?" and hold him to it until he says, "I know that God has
heard me." Then have him read the 15th verse and ask him, "If
you know that God has heard you, what further do you know?"
Hold him to it until he says, "I know that I have the petition that I
asked of Him." Then ask him, "What do you know you have received?" and hold him to it until, resting upon the simple naked
promise of God's Word, he can say, "I know I have received the
Holy Ghost." Many are waiting for certain ecstatic experiences of
which they have heard others speak. In dealing with an inquirer,
do not deny the reality of these experiences, for they doubtless
are real in many instances, but show the inquirer that there are
no such experiences described in the Bible, that the manifestations of having received the Holy Spirit mentioned in the Bible
are a new joy and peace in Christ,

> "But the fruit of the Spirit is love, joy, peace, longsuffering, gentleness,
> goodness, faith, meekness, temperance: against such there is no law." Gal.
> 5:22, 23,

a new and clearer knowledge of Christ,

> "But when the Comforter is come, whom I will send unto you from the
> Father, even the Spirit of truth, which proceedeth from the Father, he
> shall testify of me." Jno. 15:26,

and especially new power in service for Christ,

> "And, being assembled together with them, commanded them that they
> should not depart from Jerusalem, but wait for the promise of the Father,
> which, saith he, ye have heard of me. For John truly baptized with water;
> but ye shall be baptized with the Holy Ghost not many days hence.
> "But ye shall receive power, after that the Holy Ghost is come upon
> you: and ye shall be witnesses unto me both in Jerusalem, and in all
> Judea, and in Samaria, and unto the uttermost part of the earth." Acts
> 1:4, 5, 8.
> "And when they had prayed, the place was shaken where they were as-
> sembled together; and they were all filled with the Holy Ghost, and they
> spake the word of God with boldness. And the multitude of them that
> believed were of one heart and of one soul: neither said any of them
> that ought of the things which he possessed was his own; but they had
> all things common. And with great power gave the apostles witness of the
> resurrection of the Lord Jesus: and great grace was upon them all." Acts
> 4:31–33.

Also make it clear to the inquirer that the manifestations that result from receiving the Holy Spirit are to be expected not before
we believe, but after we believe, after we take by simple faith
God's Word. God's way is not first experience and then faith, but
first faith resting upon the naked Word of God, and then experience, "Believe *that ye have received,* and ye shall have."

XI. Christians who do not have victory in their Christian life.

There are many professed Christians, and doubtless many
who are really saved people, whose lives seem to be lives of constant defeat and discouragement. In dealing with such a person
seek to find out what is the cause of defeat. It will be found in one
or more of the following points:

1. *Because they have not learned to rest absolutely in the
finished work of Christ for pardon and for peace.* The church is full
of people who are looking to something that they themselves can
do to find acceptance before God. No one can have a clear, satisfactory and victorious Christian experience who has not learned
to rest entirely in the finished work of Christ for pardon. If this is
found to be the cause of failure, use Is. 53:6, Gal. 3:13, II Cor.
5:21 and similar passages, to show that our sins are pardoned not
on account of anything that we have done or can do, but on the
account of what Jesus Christ did when He bore our sins in His own
body on the Cross.

Next show the inquirer that the pardon and peace thus pur-
chased by the atoning blood of Christ, become ours on the simple
condition of our believing on Christ. To show this, use the following passages:

"Therefore *being justified by faith* we have peace with God through our
Lord Jesus Christ." Rom. 5:1.
"But to him that worketh not, but believeth on him that justifieth the
ungodly, *his faith is counted for righteousness.*" Rom. 4:5.
"But now the righteousness of God without the law is manifested, being
witnessed by the law and the prophets; even the righteousness of God
which is by faith of Jesus Christ unto all and upon all them that believe:
for there is no difference: for all have sinned, and come short of the glory
of God; *being justified freely by his grace* through the redemption that is
in Christ Jesus: whom God hath set forth to be a propitiation through
faith in his blood, to declare his righteousness for the remission of sins
that are past, through the forbearance of God; to declare, I say, at this

time his righteousness: that he might be just, and *the justifier of him which believeth in Jesus.*" Rom. 3:21–26.

"And be found in him, *not having mine own righteousness,* which is of the law, *but that which is through the faith of Christ,* the righteousness which is of God by faith." Phil. 3:9.

In the last passage the Revised version brings out the thought more clearly than the Authorized.

2. *Because they have not surrendered absolutely to the will of God.* This is the cause of failure in a very large proportion of cases. If this is found to be the cause of failure in any specific case, use Acts 5:32, and Rom. 6:13, 19:

"Neither yield ye your members as instruments of unrighteousness unto sin: but *yield yourselves unto God,* as those that are alive from the dead, and your members as instruments of righteousness unto God.

"I speak after the manner of men because of the infirmity of your flesh: for as ye have yielded your members servants to uncleanness and to iniquity unto iniquity; even *so now yield your members servants to righteousness* unto holiness." Rom. 6:13, 19.

3. *Because of neglect of the study of the Word.* If this is the case, use I Pet. 2:2, Ps. 119:11 and Eph. 6:17:

"Thy word have I hid in mine heart, that I might not sin against thee." Ps. 119:11.

"And take the helmet of salvation, and the sword of the Spirit, which is the word of God." Eph. 6:17.

4. *Because of neglect of prayer.* Where this is the case, use I Thess. 5:17, Luke 22:40 and Is. 40:29–31:

"And when he was at the place, he said unto them, *Pray that ye enter not into temptation.*" Luke 22:40.

5. *Because of failure to constantly confess Christ before men.* The one who would lead a victorious Christian life must be constantly witnessing for Christ. Make this very plain, and for this purpose use Matt. 10:32, 33:

"Whosoever therefore shall confess me before men, him will I confess also before my Father which is in heaven. But whosoever shall deny me before men, him will I also deny before my Father which is in heaven."

6. *Because of neglect to work for Christ.* One who would lead a victorious life must be constantly at work for the Master. If the cause of failure is at this point, use Matt. 25:29:

"For unto every one that hath shall be given, and he shall have abundance: but from him that hath not shall be taken away even that which he hath."

Explain its meaning by the context. The evident meaning of the passage is that one who uses the talents that he has in the Master's service will get more, but the one who neglects to use the talents he has will lose even those.

7. *Because they have not received the Holy Spirit.* There are very many to-day who are leading lives of constant failure where they might be leading lives of constant victory, simply because they do not even so much as know that it is the privilege of the individual believer to be filled with the Holy Spirit. If this is the case, use Eph. 5:18, the last half of the verse, and Gal. 5:16, 22, 23:

"This I say then, Walk in the Spirit, and ye shall not fulfill the lust of the flesh.

"But the fruit of the Spirit is love, joy, peace, longsuffering, gentleness, goodness, faith, meekness, temperance: against such there is no law."

Then show the inquirer how to receive the Holy Spirit as explained under the former heading.

CHAPTER XV

SOME HINTS AND SUGGESTIONS FOR PERSONAL WORK

A few general suggestions that will be helpful to the personal worker remain to be made.

I. As a rule, choose persons to deal with of your own sex.

There are, of course, exceptions to this rule. One should always be looking to the Holy Spirit for His guidance as to whom to approach, and He may lead us to one of the opposite sex, but unless there is clear guidance in the matter, it is quite generally agreed among those who have had much experience in Christian work that, on the whole, women usually do the most satisfactory work with women, and men with men; especially is this true of the young. It is always a bad sign when a young man is always looking for women to deal with, and a young woman looking for young men to deal with. Many exceedingly unfortunate complications have risen in actual life from young men trying to lead young women to Christ, and vice versa. Of course, an elderly, motherly woman will oftentimes do excellent work with a young man or boy, and an elderly, fatherly man will sometimes do good work with a young woman or girl.

II. As a rule, choose persons to deal with of about your own age.

A young man as a rule can get hold of young men better than any one else can and a man of mature years can handle a man of his own age better than a young man, or better even than an old man. It is not wise usually for a young and inexperienced person to approach one very much older and maturer and wiser than himself, on such an important subject as this. The older person naturally looks with a good deal of distrust, if not contempt, upon those much younger than himself. There are, of course, exceptions even to this rule. Frequently a man who has gained wisdom by years, and who has the confidence of people, can do excellent work with a young man or boy. As a rule people do the best work with people of their own class, educated men with educated men, business men with business men, workingmen with workingmen, women of position with women of similar position to themselves. There are many exceptions to this. Many a servant girl has been known to lead her mistress to Christ, and many a laboring man his employer.

III. Whenever it is possible, deal with a person alone.

No one likes to open his heart freely to another on the most personal and sacred of all subjects, when there are others present. Many will from mere pride defend themselves in a false position when others are present, who would freely admit their error or sin or need if they were alone with you. It is far better for a single worker to deal with a single unconverted person, than for several workers to deal with an inquirer, or a single worker to deal with several inquirers. Nothing can be more unfortunate than for a number of workers to swarm around one poor individual who is trying to find the way of life. If such an individual is a person of any independence of character, he is very likely to feel that he is being hectored and bothered, and for that very reason take an attitude of opposition. If you have several to deal with, it is better if possible to take them one by one. Workers often find that they have made no headway while talking to several at once, but by taking the individuals off by themselves they soon succeed in leading them one by one to Christ. Where two unsaved people are being dealt with at once, oftentimes each is afraid of the other, and they bolster one another up in their false position.

IV. Let your reliance be wholly in the Spirit of God and in the Word of God. Have no confidence in yourself.

One of the greatest hindrances to successful personal work is self-confidence. But while there should be no self-confidence, there should be boldness, boldness that comes from believing in the power of the Holy Ghost, and in the power of the Word of God. No matter with whom you are dealing, or how stubborn he may be, never forget that the Spirit of God and the Word of God have power to break the hardest heart. Be always looking to the Spirit to produce conviction of sin, and expect Him to do it, but let your whole dependence be in Him, and in His Word alone.

V. Have the one with whom you are dealing read the passage himself.

Do not content yourself with merely reading passages from the Bible, much less with merely quoting them. In this way the truth finds an entrance into the heart through the eye as well as through the ear. It is remarkable how much deeper an impression the Word of God oftentimes makes when it is actually seen with the eyes, than it does when it is merely heard with the ears. Sometimes it is well to have a marked Bible, with the word that you wish especially to impress marked in some striking way so that it will catch the eye, and thus the mind and heart of the reader.

VI. It is oftentimes well to use but a single passage of Scripture.

One verse of Scripture iterated and reiterated will be burned into the memory and will haunt the one with whom you are dealing long after you have left them. I have known a passage to haunt a man for weeks and finally result in his conversion. Do everything in your power to drive it home and clinch it so that the one with whom you are dealing cannot forget it, but will hear it ring in his memory long after your voice has ceased.

Dr. Ichabod Spencer tells in his "Pastoral Sketches" of how he dealt with a young man who had many difficulties. Dr. Spencer kept continually quoting the passage, "Now is the accepted time, now is the day of salvation." The young man tried to get Dr. Spencer off onto something else, but over and over again he kept saying the words, "Now is the accepted time, now is the day of salvation." The young man returned the next day rejoicing in the Lord, and thanking Dr. Spencer that he had "hammered" him with that text. The words kept ringing in his ears during the night, and he could not rest until he had settled the matter by accepting Christ.

It is a good thing when a person can point to some definite verse in the Word of God, and say, "I know on the authority of that verse that my sins are forgiven, and that I am a child of God." Indeed it is well never to let persons go until they can point you definitely to the verse in God's Word upon which they rest their hope of salvation. Be sure that they grasp it, so that if Satan comes to them when they are alone, and asks them how they know that they are saved, they can open their Bible to that verse, and put their finger upon it and defy Satan in all his wiles.

There are times, however, when a powerful effect is produced by piling up passages along some line until the mind is convinced and the heart conquered. Especially is this true in showing people their need of a Saviour, and showing them Jesus as the Saviour that they need.

VII. Always hold the person with whom you are dealing to the main point of accepting Christ.

If he wishes to discuss outside questions, such as the claims of various denominations, or the mode of baptism, or theories of future punishment, or fine points about the higher criticism, or any other question than the central one of his need of a Saviour, and Christ the Saviour that he needs, tell him these questions are important to take up in their right place and time, but the time to settle them is after he has settled the fundamental question of accepting or rejecting Christ. Many a case has been lost by an inexperienced and foolish worker allowing himself to be involved in a discussion of some side issue which it is utter folly to discuss with an unregenerated person.

VIII. Be courteous.

Many well-meaning but indiscreet Christians by their rudeness and impertinence repel those whom they would win to Christ. It is quite possible to be at once perfectly frank and perfectly courteous. You can point out to a man his awful sin and his need of a Saviour without insulting him. Your words may be very searching, while your manner is very gentle and winning, indeed the more gentle and winning your manner is, the deeper your words will go, for they will not stir up the opposition of those with whom you are dealing. Some workers approach those with whom they wish to work in such a manner that the latter at once assume the defensive, and clothe themselves with an armor that it is impossible to penetrate.

IX. Avoid unwarranted familiarities with those with whom you deal.

I have seen many workers lay their hands upon the shoulders of those with whom they are dealing, or even put their arms around them. Now there are cases in which that is proper and wise. If a man is dealing with an old wrecked and ruined drunkard who thinks he has not a friend in the world, it may be well to place your hand upon his shoulder, or over his shoulder, but one needs to be exceedingly cautious about these matters. A man of fine sensitiveness is repelled when a stranger takes any familiarities with him. This is even more true of a lady of good breeding. I have even seen a male worker so indiscreet as to lay his hand upon a lady's shoulder. There is no place where good breeding counts for more than in personal work.

X. Be dead in earnest.

Only the earnest man can make the unsaved man feel the truth of God's Word. It is well to let the passage we would use with others first sink deep into our own souls. I know of a very successful worker who has for a long time used the one passage, "Prepare to meet thy God," with every one with whom she has dealt. But that passage has taken such complete possession of her own heart and mind that she uses it with tremendous effect. A few passages that have thoroughly mastered us are much better than many passages that we have mastered from some text book.

One of the great needs of the day is men and women who are thoroughly in earnest, who are completely possessed with the great fundamental truths of God's Word. The reader of this book is advised to ponder upon his knees such of the passages suggested in it as he decides to use, until he himself feels their power. We read of Paul that he "ceased not to warn every one night and day with tears." (Acts 20:31.) Genuine earnestness will go further than any skill learned in a training class or from the study of such a book as this.

XI. Never lose your temper when trying to lead a soul to Christ.

How many a case has been lost by the worker losing his temper. Some persons are purposely exasperating, but even such may be won by patient perseverance and gentleness: they certainly cannot be won if you lose your temper, nothing delights them more, or gives them more comfort in their sin. The more irritating they are in their words and actions, the more impressed they will be if you return their insults with kindness. Oftentimes the one who has been the most insufferable will break down in penitence. One of the most insulting men I ever met afterward became one of the most patient, persistent and effective of workers.

XII. Never have a heated argument with one whom you would lead to Christ.

Heated arguments always come from the flesh and not from the Spirit. (Gal. 5:20, 22, 23.) They arise from pride, and unwillingness to let the other person get the best of you in argument. If you care more about winning him to Christ than you do about winning your case, you will often let the other man think that he has the best of the argument, absolutely refusing to argue. If the one with whom you are talking has mistaken notions that must be removed before he can be led to Christ, show him his error quietly and pleasantly. If the error is not on an essential point, refuse to discuss it at all, and hold the person to the main question.

XIII. Never interrupt any one else who is dealing with a soul.

Too much emphasis cannot be laid upon this point. You may not think the other is doing the work in the wisest way, but if you can do any better, bide your time, and you will have the opportunity. Many an unskilled worker has had some one at the very point of decision, when some meddler, who thought he was wiser, has broken in and upset the work. Do not even stand by one who is talking to another and listen to what he is saying. Incalculable mischief may be done in this way. The thought of the one who is being dealt with is distracted, his heart is closed up, and a case that might have been won is lost.

On the other hand, do not let others interrupt you. Of course, sometimes it is not possible to altogether prevent it, but stop the interruption just as soon as possible. Just a little word plainly but courteously spoken will usually prevent it, but at any cost insist upon being left alone.

XIV. Don't be in a hurry.

One of the commonest and gravest faults in Christian work to-day is haste. We are too anxious for immediate results, and so we do superficial work. It is very noticeable how many of those with whom Christ dealt came out slowly; Nicodemus, Joseph, Peter, and even Paul (though the final step in his case seems very sudden) were cases in point. It was three days even after the personal appearance of Jesus to Paul on the way to Damascus, before the latter came out clearly into the light and openly confessed Christ. (Acts 22:16.) One man with whom slow but thorough work has been done, and who at last has been brought out clearly for Christ and who knows just where he stands and what to do, is better than a dozen with whom hasty work has been done, who think they have accepted Christ, when in reality they have not. It is often a wise policy to plant a truth in a man's heart and leave it to work. The seed on rocky ground springs up quickly, but withers as quickly.

XV. Get the person with whom you are dealing on his knees before God.

This rule has exceptions. Sometimes it is not possible to get the person to kneel, and sometimes it is not wise; but it is wonderful how many difficulties disappear in prayer, and how readily stubborn people yield when they are brought into the very presence of God Himself. I remember talking with a young woman in an inquiry room for about two hours, and making no apparent headway, but when at last we knelt in prayer, in less than five minutes she was rejoicing in our Saviour. Sometimes it is well to have a few words of prayer before you deal with an individual at all, but of course this is not at all wise in many cases; however, in almost every case it is wise if the person is willing to pray, to have a few words of prayer before you close. If the way of life has been made perfectly clear to the inquirer, have him also lead in prayer. There are those who object to getting an unsaved person to pray, but there is clear Bible warrant for it. Cornelius was not a saved man. This is perfectly clear from Acts 11:14, nevertheless he was sincerely seeking the light, and God sent him word that his prayers had come up for a memorial before Him. Now, any one who is honestly seeking light, even though he has not as yet that knowledge of Jesus that brings salvation, is in practically the same position as Cornelius, and one of the best things to do is to get that one to pray. It is certainly right for a sinner seeking pardon through the atoning blood to pray. (Luke 18:13, 14.) Some may say, "One who has no faith has no right to pray." But such a one has faith, his prayer is the first evidence of that faith. (Rom. 10:13, 14.)

XVI. Whenever you seem to fail in any given case, go home and pray over it and study it to see why you failed. Never give up a case because of one failure.

If you have been at a loss to know what Scripture to use, study this book to see the different classes we meet and how to deal with them, and find out where this person belongs and how to deal with him, and then go back if you can, and try again. In any case you will be better prepared for the next case of the same kind. The greatest success in this work comes through many apparent defeats. It will be well to frequently study these hints and suggestions, and see if your failure has come through neglect of them. But be sure to take to God in prayer the case in which you yourself have failed.

XVII. Before parting with the one who has accepted Christ, be sure to give him definite instructions as to how to succeed in the Christian life.

These instructions will be found at the close of Chapter V. It is well to give these instructions in some permanent form. For this purpose two tracts have been written by the author of this book, one called "The Christian Life Card," and the other "How to Make a Success of the Christian Life." Either of these can be secured from the Bible Institute Colportage Association, Chicago.

XVIII. When you have led any one to Christ, follow him up and help him in the development of his Christian life.

There is nothing sadder in Christian work to-day than the number who are led to Christ, and then neglected. Such are almost certain to get on very poorly. No greater mistake could be possible. The work of following up those who are converted is as important as the work of leading them to Christ, and as a rule no one can do it so well as the person who has been used in their conversion.

All the methods of dealing in personal work, given in the foregoing chapters, will suggest texts and lines of thought for helpful sermons.